SWIFT'S
RHETORICAL ART

A Study in Structure and Meaning

BY MARTIN PRICE

Southern Illinois University Press

CARBONDALE AND EDWARDSVILLE

Feffer & Simons, Inc.

LONDON AND AMSTERDAM

Library of Congress Cataloging in Publication Data

Price, Martin, 1920–
   Swift's rhetorical art.
   (Arcturus books, AB 113)
   First published in 1953 by Yale University Press,
New Haven, which was issued as v. 123 of Yale studies
in English.
   1. Swift, Jonathan, 1667–1745. I. Title.
II. Series: Yale studies in English, v. 123.
[PR3728.S8P7 1973]   828'.5'09   73–7764
ISBN 0–8093–0646–8

ARCT
URUS
BOOKS ®

To Mary

Preface

There is a consistency in Swift's work that can be traced from the simplest to the most complex form, from the elements of diction and syntax in the sermons and tracts to the rhetorically ordered symbolism of *A Tale of a Tub* and *Gulliver's Travels*. This has often been discussed as the consistency of a strong personality, but we can measure the strength of the personality and understand its nature most successfully when we have examined the kinds of meaning in which it finds expression. This essay is concerned, therefore, with structure in Swift's works as it serves to create meaning—and particularly such meaning as redirects attitudes.

The term "rhetoric," as I have used it in the title, is meant to include the traditional art of persuasion as well as our recent concern with "the architecture of communication, its structure and ordonnance" (Arthur M. Clark). The art of persuasion has always required use of language more complex than that of simple factual description. In its simultaneous satisfaction of several ends, rhetoric, like architecture, becomes a problem of design, whatever else it may be. I have tried to trace some of Swift's typical designs and to see in what way they are necessary to his meaning.

The later chapters of this book deal increasingly with the large themes of Swift's major works and the last with his work as a whole. It is always dangerous to read an author's separate works as parts of one great life-work. We are tempted to overlook the change of attitude and shifts of attention of the author; even more, we tend to slight the internal necessity of a single work and to read it as another example of what can be found in all the rest. But as long as these dangers are kept in mind we may learn a great deal. In defining the meanings which are common to several works we may learn to see in its full generality the meaning of each, to perceive the wider suggestions of a work which, taken alone, may seem fairly limited. Such generalized meanings may seem thin as abstracted themes, but as we trace them back through the works they may yield clearer principles of structure and, as a result, more significance in concrete details.

I have tried to present Swift's attitudes sympathetically. This does not mean that there is not much in them to criticize (or even to translate into different terms). But it seems hopeless to embark on such criticism until we have come to some general agreement about what Swift said. Few writers have been so strongly attacked upon such irrelevant grounds. One can only hope that further study of Swift's methods will make his meanings in some measure demonstrable. This essay is offered in the hope that it may contribute a useful emphasis to an adequate reading of Swift and that it may suggest some new relations between his work and that of other periods, including our own.

The text of Swift's prose works is still in process of being newly edited by Herbert Davis. I have made use of his edition for quotation (with a few slight changes in spelling and punctuation) wherever it was available; for the rest, I have used the Temple Scott text. References are generally given to both editions where possible. In the case of the *Examiner* papers, for example, I have followed Davis' method of numbering and (old-style) dating, but I have given page references to Temple Scott's text as well. In other cases, I have used the short title given by Temple Scott as more familiar or more convenient. The following cue titles are used in the notes:

> HD: *The Prose Writings of Jonathan Swift,* ed. Herbert Davis (Oxford, Blackwell, 1939———).
>
> TS: *The Prose Works of Jonathan Swift,* ed. Temple Scott (London, Bell, 1897–1908).
>
> *Correspondence: The Correspondence of Jonathan Swift,* ed. F. E. Ball (London, Bell, 1910–14).
>
> *Poems: The Poems of Jonathan Swift,* ed. Harold Williams (Oxford, Clarendon Press, 1937).
>
> *Letters to Ford: The Letters of Jonathan Swift to Charles Ford,* ed. David Nichol Smith (Oxford, Clarendon Press, 1935).

In its original form, this essay was submitted as a dissertation for the degree of Doctor of Philosophy at Yale University. I am grateful to several persons who have read all or part of this essay in its present form or in earlier drafts—Cleanth Brooks, Joel Dorius, Frank H. Ellis, Laurence A. Michel, and Charles T. Prouty—although I would not want their kindness to be repaid with any attribution of responsibility. At each stage of planning and writing I have been helped by discussions with Harold D. Kelling, as I have by the chance to read his unpublished work on Swift. Finally, I wish to record a special debt to Benjamin C. Nangle, who has read this essay at each stage and has finally seen it through the press; to W. K. Wimsatt Jr., who was a most careful reader of the first draft; to Maynard Mack, who directed the dissertation upon which this essay is based and provided help through more than the usual number of dark moments. As for my wife's help, its dimensions can hardly be suggested by what it has produced.

M. P.

Branford College, Yale University.
August, 1952

Contents

I

The Rhetorical Background

THE ATTACK UPON RHETORIC

"PROPER Words in proper Places, makes the true Definition of a Stile: But this would require too ample a Disquisition to be now dwelt on." There Swift left the matter, with at least the assurance that he did not take his own terms to be self-explanatory.[1] What strikes us most sharply in this epigram is its negation. The terms Swift allows himself are vague and bare. Style is something to be defined in a simple generality which demands no learning and encourages no ingenuity. Propriety may involve considerable artifice, as we shall have occasion to see, but it decrees functionality above all and banishes the otiose charm which may tempt the conscious stylist. To see why Swift's terms should stress exclusion and say so little that is positive we must look back upon the rhetorical tradition which he inherited. The shift in style which marks the seventeenth century has been widely discussed. If we review it again here it is to see better the meaning of those terms which Swift could use with elliptical familiarity in his own day.

The central tradition in which Swift grew was an antirhetorical one. Its distrust of rhetoric was, of course, a distrust of one kind of rhetoric, and its distrust of the old gave motive and form to a new rhetoric which emerged in full maturity, secure and unquestioned, in the Augustan age. The distrust of rhetoric cannot be limited to the leaders of the new science or to those who fell under their influence; if we find it in Bacon and Sprat, we find it as well in Temple and South. The issues at stake are broader than any of the fields in which particular engagements were fought. We may see each front as part of the same war, and we may recognize that, as in many wars, allies are joined less by common beliefs than by common interests.

Traditional loyalties were still powerful and could be invoked to win men to a cause. But they were claimed by opposing sides and used as sanctions for hostile interests. The conflicts of the age were at least in part a competition for these sanctions. As a result there arose a profoundly critical view of the uses to which sanctifying terms were put. In some cases the terms themselves were attacked; in others they were made

---

1. *Letter to a Young Clergyman*, HD, ix, 65 (TS, iii, 201–2). The full title is *A Letter to a Young Gentleman, Lately Entered into Holy Orders*.

suspect as the likeliest means by which ambitious men might mask their true selfishness and make dupes of their fellows. The divisions in church and state, and in the commonwealth of learning, all bred motives for using words as slogans or shibboleths. "Men create oppositions which are not," wrote Bacon, "and put them into new terms so fixed, as whereas the meaning ought to govern the term, the term in effect governeth the meaning." [2] Beside this we can set Swift's remarks a century later: "there is one darling Inclination of Mankind, which usually affects to be a Retainer to Religion, although she be neither its Parent, its God-mother, or its Friend; I mean the Spirit of Opposition, that lived long before Christianity, and can easily subsist without it." [3] Between the two statements lies the work of Hobbes, his picture of man as restlessly acquisitive, "continually in competition for Honour and Dignity." [4] One can trace through the century the attempt to meet this threat to all mean-ings and all hope of peaceful agreement. For Hobbes the solution lay in the surrender of individual liberty to an absolute sovereign, whose orderly rule might at least secure men from each other and free them from the terrors of unlimited competition. For Dryden the religious solution had much in common with Hobbes' political order; where "dis-cord cannot end without a last appeal" the appeal must be made to a church "undivided, so from errors free." [5] For others the distrust of institutions was too great to permit such submission. Instead they sought to limit the sense of the terms which encourage controversy and to limit in a similar way the power that each competing interest might acquire. The state was a balance of powers, the church was a middle way. Words, finally, were to be defined within workable limits; where this could not be done, one unlimited word was set against its contrary—"Self-love, to urge, and Reason, to restrain." [6] The typical solution of the conflicts of the seventeenth century is the difficult, unsteady, exacting Augustan ideal of compromise.

This compromise could be achieved only as old rhetorical patterns were discredited. The long process of overthrowing the "witty logicians" of the seventeenth century might be said to have begun with Bacon. He, at least, did more than any other man to shape the incidental view of rhetoric held by men primarily interested in science or religion. He did much, in fact, to translate into the terms of his age the perennially lively Platonic attack upon rhetoric. The attack recurs in each age that feels

2. Francis Bacon, "Of Unity in Religion," *Essays or Counsels Civil and Moral,* in *The Philosophical Works of Francis Bacon,* ed. John F. M. Robertson (London, Rout-ledge, 1905), p. 739. All page references for Bacon are to this edition.

3. *An Argument against Abolishing Christianity,* HD, II, 34 (TS, III, 15).

4. Thomas Hobbes, *Leviathan,* Pt. II, chap. xvii.

5. John Dryden, *The Hind and the Panther,* Pt. II, lines 941, 1103, in *Poetical Works,* ed. George R. Noyes (Boston and New York, Houghton Mifflin, 1909).

6. Alexander Pope, *An Essay on Man,* ed. Maynard Mack (London, Methuen, 1950; New Haven, Yale University Press, 1951), Epistle II, line 54.

heightened confidence in its approach to truth by a more direct and less fallible means. Bacon, like Plato, regarded the power of the imagination in rhetoric as potentially subversive of rational thinking and writing. True, imagination could be used by divine grace to lead us beyond reason in parables and visions; but, used by men, it could lead too readily to complacent rationalization. The mind is lazy and more willingly embraces those "vulgar notions" which confirm its preconceptions than it labors after difficult truths. By adapting nature to accord with these vulgar notions the master of rhetoric gains an easy victory over those who would correct traditional error. The place for vulgar notions, for Bacon, is in "sciences founded on opinions and dogmas," for "in them the object is to command assent to the proposition not to master the thing." [7] Bacon, then, contrasts the rhetoric which succeeds in disputation with the science which avoids disputation. The moral reordering of experience is based upon "opinions and dogmas," whereas the discovery of causes is a search for facts. The old dispensation is for the "cultivation," the new for the "invention," of knowledge. [8]

The love of disputation, moreover, blinds men to truth. A man "more readily believes" what he "had rather were true." The mind is easily comforted by the familiar, however misleading the analogies which make it feel at home. Therefore, Bacon warns, "let every student of nature take this as a rule—that whatever his mind seizes and dwells upon with peculiar satisfaction is to be held in suspicion." [9] His view of the mind as incorrigibly weak has strong moral overtones. They are more apparent when Bacon likens the dupes of imagination to the Israelites in the desert "that would fain have returned *ad ollas carnium,* and were weary of manna; which, though it were celestial, yet seemed less nutritive and comfortable." [1] Through Bacon's work and through that of his followers rings the praise of industry. Rhetorical plausibility breeds only lazy pride. Man is always tempted by flattery; Bacon's demons "flatter the understanding by conformity with preconceived notions." [2]

The most striking statement in Bacon of this contrast is also of special interest for a reader of Swift:

> Those who have handled sciences have been either men of experiment or men of dogmas. The men of experiment are like the ant; they only collect and use: the reasoners resemble spiders, who make cobwebs out of their own substance. But the bee takes a middle course, it gathers its material from the flowers of the garden and of the field, but trans-

---

7. Bacon, *Novum Organum,* Bk. I, aphorisms xxviii, xxix, p. 262.
8. *Ibid.,* Preface, p. 257.
9. *Ibid.,* Bk. I, aphorisms xlix, lviii, pp. 267, 269.
1. Bacon, *Of the Advancement of Learning,* Bk. II, 111. Bacon is describing men in general in their inclination to "knowledges that are drenched in flesh and blood."
2. Bacon, *Novum Organum,* Preface, p. 257.

forms and digests it by a power of its own. Not unlike this is the true business of philosophy: for it neither relies solely or chiefly on the powers of the mind, nor does it take the matter which it gathers from natural history and mechanical experiments and lay it up in the memory whole, as it finds it; but lays it up in the understanding altered and digested. Therefore from a closer and purer league between these two faculties, the experimental and the rational (such as has never yet been made) much may be hoped.[3]

Here we can see Bacon's "true and lawful marriage between the empirical and the rational faculty." Bacon's interest is in the "middle axioms," those generalizations which are more than common sense and less than speculative hypothesis, for "the middle are the true and solid and living axioms, on which depend the affairs and fortunes of men." [4] Above these middle axioms more general hypotheses are necessary but not unduly abstract ones—"notional and without solidity." The test of an axiom is in its use; thus the logical syllogism confirms induction by submitting its conclusions to the test of application. The rhetorical syllogism, however, achieves its end by gaining assent, which may or may not be rational. The framing of the rhetorical syllogism, moreover, requires the use of a middle term which is familiar to the audience and accords with vulgar notions.[5] Rhetoric, at best "insinuative reason," is thus fundamentally at odds with scientific method. "For the end which this science of mine proposes is the invention not of argument but of arts. And as the intention is different, so accordingly is the effect: the effect of the one being to overcome an opponent in argument, of the other to command nature in action." [6]

Swift in *The Battle of the Books* can ignore the ant, for he makes something different of the spider and the bee. The spider is now the modern in his insular pride—whether of self, sect, or age—who "by a lazy Contemplation of four Inches round; by an overweening Pride, which feeding and engendering on itself, turns all into Excrement and Venom, producing nothing at last, but Flybane and a Cobweb." This

3. *Ibid.*, Bk. I, aphorism xcv, p. 288. The parallel to *The Battle of the Books* has been noted by R. F. Jones, "The Background of the *Battle of the Books,*" *Washington University Studies,* VII, Humanistic Series No. 2 (1920), 159 n. 112, and by Herbert Davis, *The Satire of Jonathan Swift* (New York, Macmillan, 1947), p. 23.

4. Bacon, *Novum Organum,* Bk. I, aphorism civ, p. 290.

5. See the discussion of the rhetorical syllogism in Karl Wallace, *Francis Bacon on Communication and Rhetoric* (Chapel Hill, University of North Carolina Press, 1943), pp. 92-3. On Bacon's distrust of the syllogistic method, see R. F. Jones, *Ancients and Moderns: A Study of the Background of the Battle of the Books* (St. Louis, Washington University Studies, 1936), p. 55. I am indebted throughout this chapter to this book and to the articles by R. F. Jones recently collected in *The Seventeenth Century* (Stanford, Stanford University Press, 1951).

6. Bacon, "The Plan of the Work," *The Great Instauration,* p. 249.

carries over and intensifies the tone of Bacon's criticism, but it gains intensity by stressing one quality—that of pride—and extending the charge. What Bacon charges against dogmatism and presumably rhetoric Swift turns against the individual who sees all others as enemies and values even his excrement because it is his own. We may think of the indulgent mother-goddess of Pope's *Dunciad*. Nor is the industry of Swift's bee scientific enterprise. True, it is "infinite Labor, and search, and ranging through every Corner of Nature." [7] But "Nature" is used here in a quite different sense, and the "Sweetness and Light" of the bee might well have seemed "fleshpots" to Bacon. Bacon is so anxious to free science from the obstructions of a familiar and orthodox world view that he stigmatizes as laziness the natural desire of man to make sense of his world in moral terms. If the mind shows inertia in resisting innovations, the inertia is in part a defense of the patchwork unity it has managed to give its world in order to live in it. Swift, on the other hand, sees the laziness of the mind in its refusal to submit to discipline and to cultivate taste or judgment. The common beliefs of sane men are for Swift as objective and true as Bacon's middle axioms drawn from nature. Bacon's praise of industry had become a form of cant by Swift's day. Although Swift could praise industry too—without it "life would stagnate, or indeed rather could not subsist at all" [8]—he was all too familiar with men whose uncritical industry could make them oblivious to most human values. Like Bacon, Swift admired the "true and lawful marriage between the empirical and the rational faculty," but Swift's empiricism was that of morally informed common sense, and for him the rational faculty was supported by the authority of revelation.

If Swift could share a great deal with Bacon and still change much of his emphasis, the same may be said to a lesser extent of scientific writers like Thomas Browne and Robert Boyle. The scientists in general could share Bishop Sprat's desire to "separate the knowledge of *Nature,* from the colours of *Rhetorick,* the devices of *Fancy,* or the delightful deceit of Fables." [9] Bacon was inclined to relegate the study of final causes to one of the last three categories; they had, for him, "relation clearly to the nature of man rather than to the nature of the universe." [1] Yet the general program of Bacon gained currency only through the support of many men who were seriously concerned with the study of final causes. "If we reject this enquiry," wrote Boyle, "we live in danger of being ungrateful, in overlooking those uses of things, that may give us just cause of admiring and thanking the Author of them, and of losing

7. *The Battle of the Books,* HD, 1, 150, 151 (TS, 1, 170, 172).
8. *Thoughts on Various Subjects,* TS, 1, 279.
9. Thomas Sprat, *The History of the Royal Society* (London, 1667), p. 62.
1. Bacon, *Novum Organum,* Bk. 1, aphorism xlviii, p. 266.

the benefit, relating as well to philosophy as to piety, that the knowledge of them may afford us." [2] Browne might keep distinct his reports of scientific findings and his "decent and learned admiration" of the Creator; but they are kept distinct only to be deliberately and strikingly set in juxtaposition.[3]

One of the consequences of this difference of his successors from Bacon is that they extend their distrust of rhetoric to protect all reasonable truth —whether scientific or religious—from the corruptions of imagination. Aroused by the Puritans, Browne warned against "converting metaphors into proprieties, and receiving as literal expressions obscure and involved truths." Like Swift, who affixed a passage from Irenaeus against the heretics to *A Tale of a Tub*, Browne recognized in this naïve use of scriptural metaphor the folly of the ancient heresies attacked by Epiphanius and Augustine.[4] Sprat, too, saw the shadow of ancient heresy in the "thousand intricate questions" raised in the arguments of divided sects.[5] Boyle was anxious that the "sense of Scriptures might not be depraved" and refused to allow a clear text to "evaporate into allegory" for the sake of controversy.[6] The very authority of Scripture made men resort to it for rhetorical proof, but the abuse of the method might discredit all scriptural interpretation. Man is tempted to use God's word in his own interest rather than in that of truth; this is the same laziness of mind Swift and Bacon symbolized in the spider, and the same arrogance. "In brief," Browne sums it up, "a reciprocation, or rather an inversion of the creation, making God one way, as he made us another; that is, after our image, as he made us after his own." [7] The innovator in the empire of reason whom Swift describes in the *Tale* has the "humble and civil Design" of reducing "the Notions of all Mankind, exactly to the same Length, and Breadth, and Heighth of his own." [8] The lazy complacency Bacon saw in the mind averse to novel discoveries the humanist sees as an intellectually lazy but otherwise active arrogance toward the common beliefs of other men. The Hobbesian image of predatory

2. Cited by L. T. More, *The Life and Works of the Honourable Robert Boyle* (London and New York, Oxford University Press, 1944), p. 176. See further, pp. 176–9, for a discussion of Boyle's view of final causes.

3. See G. K. Chalmers, "Sir Thomas Browne, True Scientist," *Osiris, 2* (1936), 75-6. According to Chalmers, Browne's stylistic differences from Bacon were due in part to a difference in the ends of knowledge for each; as Chalmers says (p. 76), "The decent and learned admiration of the Creator is the final aim of Browne's improvement of men's knowledge of the world." Cf. Basil Willey, *The Seventeenth Century Background* (London, Chatto and Windus, 1934), pp. 41–56.

4. Thomas Browne, *Pseudodoxia Epidemica*, Bk. I, chap. iv, in *Works*, ed. Simon Wilkin (London, 1852), I, 27, 29.

5. Sprat, *History*, p. 12.

6. Boyle, *Works* (London, 1772), I, cxl; cited by More, *The Life and Works*, p. 163. Elsewhere Boyle points to the meaningfulness of religious terms and the converse lack of clarity in many scientific ideas; see More, pp. 185–6.

7. Browne, *Pseudodoxia Epidemica*, Bk. I, chap. iii (*Works*, I, 19).

8. *A Tale of a Tub*, HD, I, 105 (TS, I, 116).

man is superimposed on the image of the controversialist, and a new image is created of the monster who rejects any surrender of self to a common good or common truth.

THE NEW RHETORIC

The full reaction against unlimited sanctions and undefined sanctifying terms can be seen in the religious controversies, where such terms were most readily available and most frequently invoked. One of the dominant themes in the criticism by which a new plain style justified itself was the attack upon metaphor and similitude. This attack took one of two forms: that metaphor was needless and irrelevant to the true ends of religious discussion; or that metaphor was unstable in meaning and divisive in its social effects. These two forms were not kept distinct in the criticism, and indeed they readily blended in an attack upon the Puritan who plumed himself on ingenious readings of obscure texts and who would not accept compromise on a generally acceptable meaning. Lavish use of metaphor, and especially of argument through metaphor, was common to both the Anglo-Catholic metaphysicals and to the much less learned nonconformists. Opposed to both kinds of extravagance, the latitudinarian movement sought to limit concern to those simple and literal truths necessary to salvation.

Chillingworth, in his reply to a Jesuit opponent, put the case sharply: "So that those places, which contain things necessary, and wherein errors were dangerous, need no infallible interpreter, because they are plain; and those that are obscure need none, because they contain not things necessary, neither is error in them dangerous." [9] This concern with simple truths accorded with a practical interest in moral teaching. The Scriptures provided a rule or law and so had to be clear and unambiguous. The test of faith for the latitudinarian was often in conduct, as the test of a theory for the empirical scientist might be its practical consequences. Just as Boyle commended the scientist who wished "not only to know Nature" but "to command her," so the latitudinarians appealed principally to the man who hoped not so much to know God as to obey Him. Both Chillingworth and Hales tended to preach moral sermons: "instead of raising matter of wonder and astonishment out of the glory and power of [Christ's resurrection] by way of use and application, to discover the issue and fruit thereof in respect to us." Hales chose to preach "the practick Resurrection, which above all concerns us; that other of *Christ* in Person, in regard of us, is but a *Resurrection in specula-*

9. William Chillingworth, *The Religion of Protestants,* in *Works* (London, 1820), I, 211.

tion." [1] The tendency of the moderate churchman anxious for agreement about common principles was to abstract from the scriptural text those moral meanings about which there could be little controversy and which could serve the cause of public order. They were content, as was Swift in his sermon on the Trinity, to leave the mysteries as a test of faith but hardly to take them as the basis of doctrine. The desire to avoid the obscure texts of Scripture was the desire to avoid being misled from God's truth by man's error. As Swift put it, "Laws penned with the utmost care and exactness, and in the vulgar language, are often perverted to wrong meanings; then why should we wonder that the Bible is so?" [2]

This fear bred a reaction against both the wit of the metaphysical divines and the enthusiasm of the less moderate Puritans. For Hales, as for Chillingworth, "the litterall, plain, and uncontroversable meaning" was all men needed "except it be where the holy Ghost himself treads us out another way." [3] There is no necessary contradiction but surely a marked difference of emphasis in Donne's words: "The literall sense is alwayes to be preserved; but the literall sense is not always to be discerned. . . . the literall sense of every place, is the principall intention of the Holy Ghost, in that place: And his principall intention in many places, is to expresse things by allegories, by figures; so that in many places of Scripture, a figurative sense is the literall sense." [4] By the time of Swift the attitude of Hales was triumphant. "I have often been offended to find," Swift could write, "St. Paul's allegories and other figures of Grecian eloquence, converted by divines into articles of faith." [5] When we compare Donne on the style of the Bible and Swift on sermon practice, we can find each stressing the virtues he might seek in both:

> the Holy Ghost in penning the Scriptures delights himself, not only with a propriety, but with a delicacy, and harmony, and melody of language; with height of Metaphors and other figures, which may work great impressions upon the Readers . . .

> When a man's Thoughts are clear, the properest Words generally offer themselves first; and his own Judgment will direct him in what Order to place them, so as they may be understood. Where Men err against this Method, it is usually on Purpose, and to shew their Learning, their Oratory, their Politeness, or their Knowledge of the World. [6]

---

1. Chillingworth, *Works,* III, 131. John Hales, "A Sermon Preached on Easter Day at Eaton Colledge," *Golden Remains* (1659; second impression, London, 1673), second sequence of pagination, p. 57.
2. *Thoughts on Various Subjects,* TS, I, 282.
3. Hales, *Golden Remains,* second sequence of pagination, p. 18.
4. From the 1624 Easter Sermon, cited by Herbert H. Umbach, "The Merit of Metaphysical Style in Donne's Easter Sermons," *ELH, 12* (1945), 117.
5. *Thoughts on Religion,* HD, IX, 262 (TS, III, 308).
6. John Donne, *LXXX Sermons* (London, 1640), lv, pp. 556(E)–557(C); cited by

The Puritan method of opening a text was much different from the metaphysical style, but the two methods had in common the sense of a special efficacy in scriptural language. The wittier plays upon words in Andrewes or Donne are an attempt to press demonstration of correspondences beyond those necessary for confirmation of doctrine, for "when the Text is pleased to expatiate, each word must needs be Doctrinall." [7] For the Puritan, in his fondness for affecting scriptural metaphor, the task was to reduce metaphor to plain doctrine. When the metaphor was obscure or the doctrine sectarian, considerable dialectic skill might be required, and this was provided in Ramist training.[8] Among the less moderate dissenting sects, however, pathetic appeal might entirely override rational argument, and words might readily become, as in Swift's *Mechanical Operation of the Spirit,* senseless sonorities, expressive only of the preacher's enthusiasm. Here is one such preacher, preparing his own way: ". . . I write infallibly, without the help of any, as it flows by inspiration or revelation from my Royal seed-spring, otherways it were no other but reason's imagination." [9]

This kind of exclusive claim to God's grace gave the dissenter a status to replace that which society might deny him. But unfortunately the zeal of the sectarian for his own cause deprived him of a sense of criticism. It may seem foolish, perhaps, to say this of painfully self-scrutinizing Puritans, and yet their scrutinies were often dramatic self-reproach more than preparation for action. The Puritan was typically a courageous wayfarer, an intrepid pilgrim.[1] Yet he was not so much a man making a deliberate choice as a stage upon which is enacted a cosmic conflict. The vast forces of good and evil seemed to work from without; the individual actor readily became the mere sufferer, more chosen than choosing. This passivity was produced by the strong emphasis upon the affec-

---

W. F. Mitchell, *English Pulpit Oratory, from Andrewes to Tillotson* (London, S. P. C. K., 1932), p. 189. *Letter to a Young Clergyman,* HD, IX, 68 (TS, III, 204).

7. Richard Stuart, *Three Sermons* (London, 1656), p. 61; cited by Mitchell, *English Pulpit Oratory,* p. 362.

8. The influence of Ramus has not yet been adequately assessed. The fullest treatment of his possible effect upon Puritan method is to be found in Perry Miller, *The New England Mind: The Seventeenth Century* (New York, Macmillan, 1939). For the Puritans Ramist training appears to have provided a method for reducing metaphor to literal sense; yet its very ease with the logic of metaphor saved figures from being dismissed as mere ornament.

9. Lawrence Clarkson, *The Lost Sheep Found* (London, 1660), p. 38; cited by William Y. Tindall, *John Bunyan Mechanick Preacher* (New York, Columbia University Press, 1934), p. 28.

1. See Kenneth B. Murdock, *Literature and Theology in Colonial New England* (Cambridge, Harvard University Press, 1949), chap. iii, pp. 67–97, esp. p. 84. Cf. also Burnet's account of Leighton: "He used often to say, that if he were to choose a place to die in, it should be an inn; it looking like a pilgrim's going home, to whom this world was all as an inn, and who was weary of the noise and confusion in it." Swift's marginal comment is, "Canting puppy." *Remarks on Burnet's History of His Own Times,* TS, X, 352.

tive aspect of religion, the ecstasy of union, the inner light; ultimately, it seemed to spring from a stress on God's transcendence, the powerlessness of the individual man unless he is chosen to be saved.

In this dependence on God's saving grace, sudden and unpredictable in its coming, the Puritan might well become irresponsible or ready for self-deception. In his dramatic emphasis so vivid is the imagery and so intense are feelings that limited precepts of conduct are easily lost or expanded into vague sentiments whose practical issue is left undetermined. "What one thing," a conformist asks the admirer of an enthusiastic sermon, "do you know, that you did not understand before, or might have understood easily, when you pleased? What things do you now understand the Reason of better than formerly?" When the dissenter protests that he has had much comfort, the reply is firm: "That's strange, when you are neither wiser nor better, as far as I can discern. One would think you should suspect them to be foolish and deceitful Comforts, because they have so little ground, except it be in your Imagination." [2] To this Swift might well add: "A plain convincing Reason may possibly operate upon the Mind both of a learned and ignorant Hearer, as long as they live, and will edify a Thousand Times more than the Art of wetting the Handkerchiefs of a whole Congregation, if you were sure to attain it." [3]

This is, of course, a caricature of actual dissenters, for it is an account of a tendency. Yet there are always men uglier than any caricature, and there were countless other tailors than John of Leyden or Lodowick Muggleton to horrify Swift with the presumption of ignorant mechanics. Not only was their speech full of Biblical phrases and echoes, as a badge of their gift, but their preaching was often given to wresting of Scripture to sectarian ends. Isaac Barrow is more moderate than many in his criticism of the dissenters' use of the Bible:

> They are not for plain sense, or plain places; but for mystical phrases, and blind expressions. They love canting, and are pleased with words which they do not understand. They are all for fancy (which they call faith, and deem spirituality), not valuing plain sense. They love not, nor care for peace; disputing and scrupling, and confounding themselves and others with perplexities, is their delight. Moderation is to them lukewarmness. [4]

2. Simon Patrick, *A Friendly Debate betwixt Two Neighbours, the One a Conformist, the Other a Non-Conformist. About Several Weighty Matters* (London, 1669), p. 110.

3. *Letter to a Young Clergyman*, HD, ix, 70 (TS, iii, 206).

4. Isaac Barrow, MS dissertation, "Of the Dissenters," printed in *Theological Works*, ed. Alexander Napier (Cambridge, 1859), ix, 585. For a general study of the attitudes toward the Puritans, especially as they throw light on Swift's work, see J. R. Maybee, "Anglicans and Non-Conformists, 1679–1704: A Study in the Background of Swift's *Tale of a Tub*" (unpublished Ph.D. dissertation, Princeton University, 1942).

The last sentence explains much of the rest. For a man living in constant spiritual crisis, any difference becomes magnified into opposition; self-justification in a company of scoffers becomes shrill, strained, vituperative. If the dissenters withdrew into their own society, enough constraint remained to make self-congratulation unpleasantly intense. To such scoffers as Samuel Parker there appeared to be neither good sense nor good will among them:

> And whoever among them can invent any new Language, presently sets up for a Man of new Discoveries; and he that lights upon the prettiest Nonsense, is thought by the ignorant Rabble to unfold new Gospel-Mysteries. And thus is the Nation shattered into infinite Factions, with senseless and phantastick Phrases; and the most fatal miscarriage of them all lies in abusing Scripture-Expressions, not only without but in contradiction to their sense.[5]

When rhetorical ingenuity was applied to public issues, it could be met most successfully by a deliberately cool, bantering style, informal, unpretentious—an antirhetorical rhetoric. It is a manner which comes easily to the confuter of sophistical rhetoric, although it may come much more happily to the Puritan Andrew Marvell or the Anglican John Eachard, for example, than to their opponents.[6] This method came close to the dialogue in Marvell's *Rehearsal Transprosed;* for, as Marvell explained, "there being no method at all in [Parker's] wild rambling talk, I must either tread just on his footsteps, or I shall be in a perpetual maze, and never know when I am come to my journey's end." [7] It was just this treading in footsteps which Simon Patrick used in *A Friendly Debate*. By means of the dialogue, Patrick forestalled the dissenters' "subterfuges" and prevented their "shifting of Phrases, and hiding themselves in a maze of Words":

> For, whereas 'tis their usual Artifice to tire out the Wise, and amuse the Simple, by rowling up and down in canting and ambiguous Expressions, he has been at the pains to ferret them from Phrase to Phrase, and never left the pursuit till they were left quite naked and defenceless, and without one crany whereby to make an escape. . . . Remove the Conformist, and then the other talks at as wise a rate, as any of their own Writers.[8]

5. Samuel Parker, *A Discourse of Ecclesiastical Politie* (London, 1670), pp. 75–6.
6. For a discussion of the new controversial manner, see Hugh MacDonald, "Banter in English Controversial Prose after the Restoration," *Essays and Studies of Members of the English Association, 32* (1946), 21–9.
7. Andrew Marvell, *The Rehearsal Transprosed,* in *The Complete Works in Verse and Prose,* ed. A. B. Grosart (London, 1873), III, 118.
8. This account of Patrick's method is Samuel Parker's, in "The Preface to the Reader," *Discourse,* p. xvi.

The dialogue provides a context of moderation, clear argument, and meaningful terms against which the vices of the nonconformist may appear as follies. Patrick's method is one of "mirth"; he makes the non-comformist ridiculous by exposing the motives which underlie his professions and by revealing the effort necessary to sustain his rationalizations:

> C. Your Sermons are chiefly about prayer, and meditation, and Communion with God, and Believing—
>
> N. C. Yes, Believing: Now you have hit my meaning.
>
> C. But I was going to add something to that word, viz. Believing, without Doing. Else you will not count it spiritual Preaching.
>
> N. C. Not if they should insist much upon Doing. For there are more Spiritual matters for Believers to be instructed in.[9]

Pride in "easy and familiar words" might often lead to oversimplification. All that was not clear and simple seemed craft or delusion. "If they have found reasons to alter their Principles, then we have done. If they have not, what reasons can they be but carnal ones, which alter their practice?" [1] This distrust of motive pervaded the discussion of such unlimited terms as "grace" and "tender conscience" when they were opposed to "morality" or "conformity." South on tender conscience sounds very much like the Trimmer on the common law: "there can be no bounds or limits put to this plea, nor any possibility of defining that just number of particulars to which it may extend." It was the combination of the unlimited meaning and the sanctified nature of these terms that created danger. Conscience, as South remarked, "commands in the name of God," however it may serve the private will.[2] If God is opposed to the state, the choice is clear: "to make Proviso's for Tender Consciences, is to abate the whole Law." [3] In the desire to retain perspicuous law the tendency to oversimplify becomes most marked. We can see it in South's implicit assumption that resistance to conformity is itself impiety: "The godly party is little better than a contradiction in the adjunct; for he who is truly godly, is humble and peaceable, and will neither make nor be of a party, according to the common sense of that word." [4] This

9. Patrick, A Friendly Debate, p. 30.

1. Ibid., p. 56. For the pride in clarity of terms, see Simon Patrick, Works, ed. Alexander Taylor (Oxford, 1858), vi, 410, and Parker, Discourse, p. 75.

2. Robert South, Sermons Preached upon Several Occasions (Oxford, 1842), ii, 177, 178.

3. Parker, Discourse, p. 269.

4. South, Sermons, ii, 151. Cf. a similar passage (ii, 179): "it is ten to one but God rather speaks in the conscience of a lawful Christian magistrate making a law, than in the conscience of any private persons whatsoever dissenting from it." For the earlier and more tolerant views of Jeremy Taylor, see T. G. Steffan, "The Social Argument against Enthusiasm (1650–1660)," University of Texas Studies in English, 21 (1941), 52–5. Important for a study of the whole period is George Williamson, "The Restoration Revolt against Enthusiasm," Studies in Philology, 30 (1933), 571–603.

reductive tendency is even more obvious in Parker. In seeking to make clear that grace and morality imply and limit each other, he would equate the two; if grace is not morality, "it can be nothing else but a cheat and enthusiasm." [5]

We can see, then, in many aspects of seventeenth-century thought, the central concern with limiting the meaning of the law. The ideal which Swift suggested in Brobdingnag of simple, short, unambiguous laws was one expression of the desire for public order. In a sense it was the most important expression of all. As South put it, "Words govern the generality of the world, who seldom go so deep as to look at things: and imposters well know how likely their cause is to succeed, if their terms can but once be admitted." [6] In every kind of rule the same stress came to prevail. The method of natural philosophy was a wedding of the empirical and rational methods, a middle way between fact and dogma. The constitutionalism of Locke and his followers established an "empire of laws, not men," and the laws held in balance the rival interests of the state. The Church of England was a middle way of decency between "the meretricious gaudiness of the Church of Rome and the squalid sluttery of fanatic conventicles"; it was the way of Martin in *A Tale of a Tub*.[7]

All these tendencies cooperated to promote a rhetoric far different from the more expansive, celebrative, hyperbolic manner of the preceding age. Terms were now to be scrutinized carefully for both their sincerity and their practical consequences. As for sincerity, we can see the tenor of Halifax' distrust: "It is fair if men can believe that their friends love them *next* to themselves, to love them *better* is too much; the Expression is so *unnatural* that it is *cloying,* and men must have no *sense,* who in this case have no suspicion." [8] As for the practical consequences, they demand clarity if they are to be realized at all and caution if they are to be what one intends or should intend. "Men do not many times consider the whole signification of words," warn the Port Royal logicians, "that is, that the words often signifie more than they seem to signifie, and that therefore they who interpret the signification, do not thoroughly unfold all the Ideas which the words imprint in the minds of the Hearers." [9]

The rhetoric which came to the fore disdained the old manner as misguided and artificial; it in turn professed to be no rhetoric at all. But

5. Samuel Parker, *A Reproof to the Rehearsal Transprosed, in a Discourse to Its Authour* (London, 1673), p. 52.

6. South, *Sermons,* II, 164.

7. [Simon Patrick], *A Brief Account of the New Sect of Latitude-Men* (London, 1662), p. 11; cited in G. R. Cragg, *From Puritanism to the Age of Reason, a Study of Changes in Religious Thought within the Church of England 1660–1700* (Cambridge, Cambridge University Press, 1950), p. 41 n. 3.

8. George Savile, First Marquess of Halifax, *The Complete Works,* ed. Walter Raleigh (Oxford, Clarendon Press, 1912), p. 111.

9. [Antoine Arnauld and Pierre Nicole], *Logic; or, the Art of Thinking* (London, 1685), p. 141.

every shift in style declares itself as a new artlessness, a return to nature. It is important to see in the new rhetoric more than the loss of a certain scope of meaning; we must see as well the freeing of one kind of meaning from a context in which it could never gain full emphasis. The clarity of the new style makes for a sharp awareness of the oppositions of terms and of the latent implications in a general term. The truth is no longer to be found in the power of unlimited terms but in the area wherein contraries overlap. The strategy of the middle way pervades all writing and makes of compromise the constantly exciting exposure of the fallacy of extremes. Because the extremes are more compelling and because the defined limits are so easy to cross, there is a new stress on responsibility, upon the vigilance which detects the sham in words and exposes their misuse. The middle way is achieved not by lukewarmness but by discipline, and this discipline involves both heart and head. As the trust in plain and simple doctrine grows, so does the feeling that no man can miss its sense except through willful neglect or brutal stupidity. Whatever his motives in rejecting his duty, the sinner lends himself to being portrayed as a dunce. It is not a peculiar discovery of Swift's age that the devil is an ass, but few ages could so lovingly demonstrate the assertion with examples of sophistry, cant, and delusion.

II

The Plain Style

"PROPER WORDS IN PROPER PLACES"

SHIFTS of style are rarely complete transformations. As a new rhetoric succeeds an old, it can hardly strip itself of all those virtues which make the old succeed. It will at most find new ways, agreeable to its central emphasis, of achieving similar ends. As Charles Williams said of the Augustans, "the strangeness that those poets drove out through the back window they let in again, formally and on a defined visit, through the front door." [1] We have seen the movement toward defined meanings and toward a more general diction that might express the practical moral sense of the Augustans. It is necessary to see as well the way in which "strangeness" is readmitted to a style that is consciously "natural." We cannot easily see this in Swift's professed theory of style; yet we need not take his words in too narrow a sense. When, for example, he praises simplicity ("without which no human performance can arrive to any great Perfection"), he seems to be attacking affectations of learning, rhetorical skill, or politeness. So he is in his *Letter to a Young Clergyman.* But in another letter to a young clergyman, written some years later, he condemns a "careless, incorrect, and improper style" and concludes: "It is your business, who are coming into the world, to put a stop to these corruptions, and recall that simplicity which in everything of value ought to be followed." [2] Simplicity is clearly not artless spontaneity. Rather, like nature, it is the norm from which man departs through perversity and which he must work to regain or restore. It is similar to the ideal of the primitive church to which Swift constantly alludes as an ecclesiastical standard or like the elusive Martin of the *Tale,* who is characterized chiefly by his recovery from the errors of both Peter and Jack. Coleridge's comments on Swift's style come as close as any to Swift's own meaning: "the manner is a complete expression of the matter, the terms appropriate, and the artifice concealed. It is simplicity in the true sense of the word." [3]

The phrase "artifice concealed" is important. The very ease and fa-

1. *The New Book of English Verse* (New York, Macmillan, 1936), p. 803.
2. *Correspondence,* v, 113 (Swift to the Rev. Henry Clarke, 12 December 1734). See also TS, x, 15.
3. *Coleridge's Miscellaneous Criticism,* ed. Thomas M. Raysor (Oxford, Clarendon Press, 1936), pp. 219-20, 224.

miliarity of the new rhetoric makes its aptness unexpectedly pointed. As Pope said, the method of propriety "gives beauty even to the minute and particular thoughts, which receive an additional advantage from those which precede or follow in their due place." [4] The couplet perhaps best reveals the way in which the regularity and seeming naturalness of form allow for a precise manipulation of parts. Minute elements of style acquire value only as they are used in a clear structure; if the structure is tight enough to use them at once in several ways, each part becomes a small miracle of design. Each feather in the Indian's crown, to use Pope's example from Dryden, becomes important because of its position in an ordered array of various feathers. In a similar way, a style may use the language of statement and still achieve sudden and surprising complexities or heightenings by its ordering of parts. It is in some such way as this that the strangeness is readmitted. For Swift, the worthwhile ends of pathetic oratory or ingenious formality might be realized by a calculated use of simple means. For Donne, the artifices of rhetoric were necessary "to trouble the understanding, to displace, and discompose and disorder the judgment." It is just this that Swift seeks to accomplish, but the rule of simplicity requires that the *surface* of the text violate expectation as little as possible.[5] Its words are not—to use one description of rhetorical figures—"manners of speaking, different and remote from the ways that are ordinary and natural . . . quite other than what we use, when we speak without passion." [6] The principal heightening of Swift's rhetoric is a heightening of propriety, a peculiar and often startling aptness of "proper places."

Swift's sermons, although they are hardly his most brilliant prose, illustrate very well the rhetoric of the plain style. In his discussion of the pagan philosophers, Swift acknowledges their justness in conceiving of a divine power and a providence. "But," he goes on, "as for a trust or dependence upon God, they would not have understood the phrase; it made no part of the profane style." [7] It is often Swift's task in the tracts to translate a moral doctrine into a "profane style"; especially is this the case in the sermons where the dual nature of man constantly

4. Alexander Pope, *Works*, ed. Whitwell Elwin and W. J. Courthope (London, 1871), VI, 34–5 (29 November 1707, to Wycherley). See Edward N. Hooker, "Pope on Wit: the *Essay on Criticism*," in R. F. Jones *et al.*, *The Seventeenth Century*, pp. 225–46, esp. p. 245.

5. Donne, *LXXX Sermons*, lxxi, p. 723(E) ; cited by Mitchell, *English Pulpit Oratory*, p. 191. See Maynard Mack, " 'Wit and Poetry and Pope': Some Observations on His Imagery," in *Pope and His Contemporaries: Essays Presented to George Sherburn*, ed. James L. Clifford and Louis A. Landa (Oxford, Clarendon Press, 1949), pp. 20–40.

6. [Bernard Lamy], *The Art of Speaking. Written in French by Messieurs du Port Royal* (London, 1696), p. 75.

7. *On the Wisdom of This World*, HD, IX, 245 (TS, IV, 176). In HD, IX, the title used is *A Sermon upon the Excellency of Christianity, in Opposition to Heathen Philosophy*.

evokes a double vision of his estate. This is most striking in the sermon *On Mutual Subjection* where Swift must assert the "extraordinary" teaching of St. Peter: "Yea, all of you be subject one to another." Acceptance of the text demands a rejection of the world's standards, and Swift's exordium is entirely devoted to making this revaluation inescapable. In a worldly view, "two Persons cannot properly be said to be subject to each other"; rather, "Subjection is only due from Inferiors to those above them." Yet *mutual* subjection is the theme, and it must not be reduced to the profane style of a bland hypocrisy, as "when our Betters are pleased to tell us they are our humble Servants, but understand us to be their Slaves." Nor may this extraordinary doctrine be translated into the common virtues of humility, charity, and patience; all of these are commendable, but in themselves they need not disturb worldly stations.[8]

The force of the sermon comes from Swift's constant insistence upon an opposition of standards. Realistic, even cynical, observations which are shocking in their lack of deference to worldly dignity serve to confirm the doctrine of St. Peter and almost to follow from it. To assure his audience that God is no "Respecter of Persons," Swift can (and by the logic of his argument seems obliged to) make biting remarks about those whom men are taught to respect:

> Princes are born with no more Advantages of Strength or Wisdom than other Men; and, by an unhappy Education, are usually more defective in both than thousands of their Subjects.

> Power, Wealth, and the like outward Advantages, are so far from being the Marks of God's approving or preferring those on whom they are bestowed, that, on the contrary, he is pleased to suffer them to be almost engrossed by those who have least Title to his Favour.[9]

These assertions, offered as sober confirmation of a theme, clearly have a function beyond that of proof. A witty reversal in the profane style is carried off as perfectly congruous with the new vision. With no straining for emphasis, Swift can introduce the bitterest charges of social injustice or corruption as matter-of-fact evidence for God's transcendent purposes.

This process of reversal works at the level of single words as well, and it demands a continual alertness. The parable of the talents prepares us for a careful shifting of terms:

8. *On Mutual Subjection,* HD, IX, 141 (TS, IV, 111–12).
9. HD, IX, 142–3, 144 (TS, IV, 112–13, 114). There is a similar passage in the sermon, *On the Martyrdom of King Charles I,* HD, IX, 228–9 (TS, III, 199–200), beginning, "There is no more inward value in the greatest emperor than in the meanest of his subjects . . ."

Now, although the Advantages which one Man possesseth more than another, may in some Sense be called his Property with respect to other Men, yet with respect to God they are, as I said, only a Trust.

The word "Advantages" abstracts from worldly honor or wealth the single element of superiority; this is to prepare for the toppling such dignities are to suffer, and the qualifying phrase "in some Sense" provides the first warning of what will happen. "Advantages" and "Property" give way to "Trust." In the next paragraph Swift moves to "Punishment":

the Princes of this World see by other Men's Eyes, but God sees all Things; and therefore whenever he permitteth his Blessings to be dealt among those who are unworthy, we may certainly conclude, that he intends them as a Punishment to an evil World, as well as to the Owners.[1]

These passages show the strangeness which can be achieved with "proper words." Swift's words are not uncommon and in themselves are neutral enough. Yet their very abstractness allows for the forceful opposition of antithesis. The opposition grows, moreover, out of the double perspective which Swift maintains throughout. The ironic ambiguity he gives to such terms as "Property," "Blessings," and particularly the final "Owners" is created by and in turn supports the central contrast, "with respect to other Men, yet with respect to God." Here the proper words are abstract enough to effect a reversal and flat enough so that the reversal is unobtrusively managed. The effect is to startle us into seeing the danger of such complacency as these words may breed.

This artful use of proper words in proper places is more obvious in a sentence near the close of the same sermon:

God sent us into the World to obey his Commands, by doing as much Good as our Abilities will reach, and as little Evil as our many Infirmities will permit.[2]

Swift is not content with a smooth and vacuous balance; a few deviations from exact symmetry achieve a more important kind of exactness. The insertion of "many" strengthens the implicit contrast between the active "reach" and the concessive "permit." As a result, the total meaning includes a strong emphasis on the inequality of the conflict and suggests the need for active effort to maintain even a balance. This is the plain style turned to considerable rhetorical effect.

Swift's use of the balanced sentence and elaborate antithesis is not infrequent in the sermons; but, unlike Johnson's more conspicuous and systematic use of them, Swift's is chiefly restricted to the summary of

1. HD, IX, 146-7 (TS, IV, 116-17).
2. HD, IX, 149 (TS, IV, 118).

a point argued at length. When this occurs at the close of a paragraph or a group of paragraphs, it often serves as the peculiarly overt and sharp statement with which Swift concludes an argument largely implicit. In his sermon on *Doing Good,* for example, he stresses the need for extending love of neighbor to love of the public and cites the ancient concept of "virtue":

> In those times it was common for men to sacrifice their lives for the good of their country, although they had neither hope or belief of future rewards; whereas, in our days, very few make the least scruple of sacrificing a whole nation, as well as their own souls, for a little present gain; which often hath been known to end in their own ruin in this world, as it certainly must in that to come.[3]

Sometimes most of a paragraph is developed through antithesis, not working back and forth between two explicit points as Johnson's might but rather introducing into each sentence an implicit contrast. The last sentence is typically the most concise and forceful of all. Here the structure turns on the contrast between imperfect human and true divine justice:

> However, *although Virtue and Innocence are no infallible Defence against Perjury, Malice, and Subornation, yet they are great Supports for enabling us to bear those Evils with Temper and Resignation;* and it is an unspeakable Comfort to a good Man under the Malignity of evil mercenary Tongues, that a few Years will carry his Appeal to an higher Tribunal, where false Witnesses, *instead of daring to bring Accusations before an all-seeing Judge, will call for Mountains to cover them.* As for earthly Judges, *they seldom have it in their Power; and, God knows, whether they have it in their Will,* to mingle Mercy with Justice; *they are so far from knowing the Hearts of the Accuser or the Accused, that they cannot know their own;* and *their Understanding is frequently biassed, although their Intentions be just.* They are often prejudiced to Causes, Parties, and Persons, through the Infirmity of human Nature, without being sensible themselves that they are so: *And therefore, although God may pardon their Errors here, he certainly will not ratify their Sentences hereafter.*[4]

If, as we have seen, proper places can include quite elaborate and artificial structures, it may be well to look more closely at the kind of words these structures require. The first is the abstract or general term which antithesis demands. As W. K. Wimsatt has said, "Not things but aspects of them can be contrasted in words. The more a writing deals with aspects as such, that is, with abstractions, the more plastic it is and shapable into

---

3. *Doing Good,* HD, IX, 233 (TS, IV, 182).
4. *On False Witness,* HD, IX, 185 (TS, IV, 166). Italics added.

the exact oppositions of antithesis. Generality and abstraction are concentration of meaning into the pure forms which admit sharp contrast." [5]
Swift, as we have seen, never relinquishes for very long the use of abstract
or general terms. Often, however, they are personified, allegorized, or
turned into metaphor:

> While Health . . . is the general Portion of the lower Sort, the Gout,
> the Dropsy, the Stone, the Cholick, and all other Diseases are con-
> tinually haunting the Palaces of the Rich and the Great, as the natural
> Attendants upon Laziness and Luxury . . . Business, Fear, Guilt,
> Design, Anguish, and Vexation are continually buzzing about the
> Curtains of the Rich and the Powerful, and will hardly suffer them to
> close their Eyes, unless when they are dozed with the Fumes of strong
> Liquors.[6]

This illustrates Swift's "fine use of the active verb," and it shows the
verb being used to elaborate a figure.[7] "Haunting" suggests the courtiers
at a levee; the mere mention of "Attendants" upon "the Rich and the
Great" is sufficient concreteness to allow Swift to return to abstract nouns.
The relevant aspects of the rich and the great are "Laziness and Luxury."
The next paragraph picks up the more general sense of "haunting" and
transforms it into a new figure of annoying insects. Both "haunting" and
"buzzing" are metaphors which carry the general idea of "troubling."
They give it precision and force, but neither metaphor is allowed to lose
its generality.

Swift frequently uses metaphorical terms of this sort, lightly asserted,
rarely carried very far: "such who had *drunk too deep* of the bad principles then prevailing," and "They did not think it sufficient to *leave*
all the errors of Popery, but *threw off* many laudable and edifying institutions of the Primitive Church." [8] Used in this way, metaphor serves some
of the same purposes as abstraction. In substituting one concrete term
for another, the metaphor implies the general term which would link the
two. The metaphors become notable instances of a general type of behavior. They become that form of generalization "in which an individual
is taken as a type, as the representative *par excellence* of an attribute." [9]

In Swift's use of abstraction and metaphor we can see two parts of the
same rhetorical program. His task is to expose in common experience

5. W. K. Wimsatt Jr., *The Prose Style of Samuel Johnson* (New Haven, Yale University Press, 1941), p. 43.
6. *On the Poor Man's Contentment,* HD, IX, 193 (TS, IV, 205).
7. The phrase is G. Wilson Knight's in "Swift and the Symbolism of Irony," *The
Burning Oracle* (London, Oxford, 1939), p. 122. Of Swift's narrative style, Knight
observes, "The plainness consists . . . in continual emphasis on noun and verb with
rejection of the *qualifying* adjectives" (p. 117).
8. *On the Martyrdom of King Charles I,* HD, IX, 224, 221 (TS, IV, 195, 192). Italics
added.
9. Hedwig Konrad, *Étude sur la métaphore* (Paris, Maurice Lavergne, 1939), p. 84.

those qualities which command immediate judgment. His terms may directly name values or represent them in metaphor. In either case, they depart suddenly from the level of neutral description or explanation toward greater abstractness or concreteness; they violate expectation. It is the use of abstraction, for example, where one expects a more concrete term that gives much of the force to this passage:

> For, pray, what would become of the Race of Men in the next Age, if we had nothing to trust to, besides the scrophulous, consumptive Productions furnished by our Men of Wit and Pleasure; when having squandered away their Vigour, Health and Estates; they are forced, by some disagreeable Marriage, to piece up their broken Fortunes, and entail Rottenness and Politeness on their Posterity? [1]

Somewhat less obvious than "Laziness and Luxury" or "Rottenness and Politeness" are the effects of Swift's frequent lists of parallel terms. They range from moral abstractions to much more specifically descriptive terms, and this very inequality of status creates an interaction. In such a list as "folly, malice, pride, cruelty, revenge, undutifulness," the very task of relating the terms placed together makes us aware of new combinations. They move toward fusion (foolish pride, cruel revenge, proud undutifulness) yet never quite settle. Where they merge more readily, as in "perfect spite, rage, and envy," the combination of general qualities creates a comparatively concrete image. Just as the terms opposed in antithesis abstract the qualities of an experience, so the abstract qualities baldly set together move toward new concreteness. Or a series of comparatively general terms may be suddenly focused in a single metaphor, as in the last words of this sentence:

> These Men can expect to hear of nothing but Terrors and Threatenings, their Sins laid open in true Colours, and eternal Misery the Reward of them; therefore no Wonder they stop their Ears, and divert their Thoughts, and seek any Amusement, rather than stir the Hell within them. [2]

Finally, in a passage from *The Drapier's Letters,* we can see the thoroughgoing cooperation of abstract and concrete:

> It is true, indeed, that within the Memory of Man, the Parliaments of *England* have *sometimes* assumed the Power of binding this Kingdom [Ireland], by Laws enacted there; wherein they were, at first, openly opposed (as far as *Truth, Reason,* and *Justice* are capable of *opposing*) by the famous Mr. *Molineaux,* an *English* Gentleman born here; as well as by several of the greatest Patriots, and *best Whigs* in *England;* but the *Love and Torrent* of Power prevailed. Indeed, the Arguments

1. *An Argument against Abolishing Christianity,* HD, ii, 30 (TS, iii, 10–11).
2. *A Sermon upon Sleeping in Church,* HD, ix, 215–16 (TS, iv, 227).

on both Sides were invincible. For in *Reason,* all *Government* without the Consent of the *Governed,* is the *very Definition of Slavery:* But in *Fact, Eleven Men well armed, will certainly subdue one single Man in his Shirt.* But I have done. For those who have used *Power* to cramp *Liberty,* have gone so far as to resent even the *Liberty* of *Complaining;* although a Man upon the Rack, was never known to be refused the Liberty of *roaring* as loud as he thought fit.[3]

Here such general terms as "Truth, Reason, and Justice" give weight to the concrete instances that follow. In the ironic opposition of "Arguments," the principle of liberty and the fact of power are set off as abstract and concrete. In the last sentence the abstract "Liberty" gains new meaning with increased concreteness: it moves from an assertion of political rights to the irrepressible pain of an otherwise thoroughly repressed victim. And how abstract or concrete is such a phrase as "Love and Torrent of Power," into which both motive and energy are compressed?

Propriety, then, for Swift is not simply a principle of exclusion. The plainness of his style comes of the rejection of expansive imagery and analogical turns, of elaborated schemes and tropes. The plainness is, however, at most a surface of conventional meaning beneath which rhetorical shaping is at work. When this shaping itself rises to the surface, we are hardly inclined to call the style plain. This sudden emergence of rhetorical import becomes more apparent as a strategy when we turn to one of the central problems of Swift's rhetoric, the task of redefinition.

Definition and Revaluation

In the competition for sanctions, each side seeks to capture those words which have wide appeal or, when that fails, to destroy those words which cannot be captured.[4] This destruction can be managed if one limits the meaning of the term and denies the relevance of the "accessory ideas" which usually accompany it. Or one can show that the term has been used so loosely as to have almost no descriptive meaning left. This second method may be carried even farther. Once the vagueness of descriptive meaning and the speciousness of a word's effect are exposed, one can make an easy inference to the possible reasons for its use. One may convert it into dramatic utterance, the cant of a schemer whose intentions are clear or of a fool whose mind is muddled. We can see Swift's use of this procedure in his reply to the dissenters' plea of "Persecution":

I have been sometimes admiring the wonderful Significancy of that Word *Persecution,* and what various Interpretations it hath acquired

3. HD, x, 62–3 (TS, vi, 114–15).
4. On the "competition for sanctions," see above, pp. 1–2.

even within my Memory. When I was a Boy, I often heard the *Presby-terians* complain, that they were not permitted to serve God in their own Way; they said, they did not repine at our Employments, but thought that all Men, who live peaceably, ought to have Liberty of Conscience, and Leave to assemble. That Impediment being removed at the Revolution, they soon learned to swallow the *Sacramental Test,* and began to take very large Steps, wherein all who offered to oppose them, were called Men of a *persecuting Spirit.* During the Time the Bill against Occasional Conformity was on Foot, *Persecution* was every Day rung in our Ears, and now at last the *Sacramental Test* itself has the same Name. Where then is this Matter likely to end, when the obtaining of one Request is only used as a Step to demand another? A Lover is ever complaining of *Cruelty* while any thing is denied him; and when the Lady ceases to be *cruel,* she is from the next Moment at his Mercy: So *Persecution,* it seems, is every Thing that will not leave it in Men's Power to *persecute others.*[5]

By tracing carefully the shifts of reference which the word has suffered, Swift makes clear its vagueness and the expediency which governs its use. Such words as "Steps" and "Impediment" serve to suggest a march to power, which moves consistently forward with each apparently local complaint. The theme of hypocritical complaint provides the fine analogy of the lover (his "Cruelty" is the dissenters' "Persecution"). But the figure of the lover also brings to the foreground the unspoken threat which lies behind the vague appeal. The dependence of true meaning upon inter-est is finally made vivid in the juxtaposition of pretended and intended "Persecution." Swift neatly converts the dissenters' use of unlimited terms into evidence of their desire for unlimited power:

> *In such a Case they talk in Tropes,*
> *And, by their Fears express their Hopes.*[6]

In the same pamphlet Swift undertakes to destroy the plea that repeal-ing the Test "will unite all Protestants against the *common Enemy.*" He begins his attack with an examination of terms: "Neither is it very clear, how far some People may stretch the Term of *common Enemy:* How many are there of those that call themselves Protestants, who look upon our Worship to be idolatrous as well as that of the *Papists,* and with great Charity put *Prelacy* and *Popery* together, as Terms convertible?" Swift goes on to recall the dissenters' intolerant persecution of others during the Commonwealth or, in Swift's terms as he lapses into the idiom

5. *A Letter concerning the Sacramental Test,* HD, II, 122 (TS, IV, 18–19). Cf. the words of the *Examiner:* "that grievous Persecution of the modern kind, called *Want of Power.*" *Examiner,* No. 30 (1 March 1710), HD, III, 97 (TS, IX, 196).

6. "Verses on the Death of Dr. Swift," *Poems,* II, 557, lines 117–18. Cf. *Examiner,* No. 24 (18 January 1710), HD, III, 67 (TS, IX, 155–6).

a dissenter might use, "in those times when the Church of *England* was *malignant.*" The next paragraph sustains the dissenter's idiom at the outset: "But this is ripping up old Quarrels long forgot; *Popery* is now the *common Enemy,* against which we must all unite." But now that Swift has brought the key term to the fore and prepared the context, he can turn the argument inside out:

> I have been tired in History with the perpetual Folly of those States who call in Foreigners to assist them against a *common Enemy:* But the Mischief was, these *Allies* would never be brought to allow that the *common Enemy* was quite subdued: And they had Reason; for it proved at last, that one part of the *common Enemy* was those who called them in; and so the *Allies* became at length the *Masters.*[7]

Once they have identified their interest with the state they have conquered, the allies can justly call enemies those who first introduced them into the state and thus subverted it. The irony of perspectives makes evident the deceptions which lie in a phrase like "common Enemy." As in the case of the persecuted lover, Swift can show the threat of ambition which vague terms are stretched to cover.

Swift's use of "they had Reason" is one of his frequent signs of the ironic turn which rests on the ambiguity of terms. In his letter to the October Club, warning against undue demands for party patronage from the Harley ministry, he dismisses the Whig precedent:

> I well remember the Clamors often raised during the Reign of that Party against the Leaders, by those who thought their Merits were not rewarded; and they had Reason on their side; because it is, no doubt, a Misfortune to forfeit *Honour* and *Conscience* for nothing.[8]

The ambiguity of "Merits" includes both its party sense of complete subjection to common interest and its usual moral sense of virtuous efforts. Both meanings are satisfied in the final explanation; in fact it is the surprise and incongruity of the explanation which emphasize the double sense of "Merits." This device of letting the same words express incompatible values is the principal method of irony. Swift's irony depends very often on the disparity between the values implied by the sanctifying term—"persecution," "moderation," "toleration," "prerogative"—and the values served by its use. The irony lies in the simultaneous presentation of the "official version" and the "real meaning" in the same

---

7. HD, II, 121–2 (TS, IV, 17, 18). Cf. the injunction in a letter to the *Examiner:* "turn the whole Mystery of Iniquity inside-out, that every Body may have a View of it." *Examiner,* No. 28 (15 February 1710), HD, III, 89 (TS, IX, 186).

8. *Some Advice . . . to the Members of the October Club,* HD, VI, 77 (TS, V, 222). For other examples of "they had Reason" or its equivalent, see TS, IX, 160, 166, 225.

term. Where the result yields an incongruity (in this last case, the complaint of unrewarded sin), the conflict of values becomes conspicuous, and the ambiguity is resolved only by undercutting the pretensions of those who use the term.[9]

The reduction of his sanctions to a vocabulary of selfish deception is perhaps the most obvious way to discredit an opponent. This is but one result of a method Swift constantly uses, the method of redefinition. Words acquire their force through a gradual process of association. Classifications are established and revised countless times before a term achieves the precision of meaning and suggestion that makes it useful. "Persecution," for example, is a term which classifies an act by placing it among innumerable cases of the slaughtering of saints or the enslaving of free men. Its suggestiveness and its emotive force depend upon a funding of traditional references to which it can be applied. The task of rhetoric is to destroy the usefulness of the term or to make it applicable in a way which supports one's own case. This may be done most easily by redefining the term in a way which does as little violence as possible to preconceptions and which seems to accord in some way with previous use. C. L. Stevenson cites a case where, in his view, the emotive meaning of a term is altered while its descriptive meaning is retained:

> Culture is only fool's gold; the true metal is imaginative sensitivity and originality.[1]

Actually, the word "culture" is here redefined descriptively as well as emotively; the speaker implies a meaning of culture which opposes it to two elements one might ordinarily consider part of culture or at least harmonious with it. The metaphorical relation is "fool's gold" to "true

9. Cf. "every under-strapper began at length to perk up and assume: he *expected a Regiment;* or, *his Son must be a Major;* or, *his Brother a Collector;* else he threatened to *Vote according to his Conscience." Examiner,* No. 19 (14 December 1710), HD, III, 37 (TS, IX, 117). Or of Marlborough: "the other Party had bid higher for him than his Friends could afford to give." *The History of the Four Last Years of the Queen,* HD, VII, 7 (TS, X, 25). This technique is made more obvious in a passage on the preceding page, HD, VII, 6 (TS, X, 24). Swift is discussing the Whig leader, Lord Somers, whom he has characterized as a man of great prudence but no true virtue. In this passage the phrases I have put into italics distinguish in each case the real prudential motive from the apparent virtuous one. The italicized phrases bring to the fore the ambiguity of the rest: "I have been assured, and heard him profess, That He was against engaging in that foolish Prosecution of Dr. Sacheverell; *as what he foresaw was likely to end in their Ruin;* That he blamed the rough Demeanor of some Persons to the Queen, *as a great Failure in Prudence;* and that, when it appeared Her Majesty was firmly resolved to enter into a Treaty of Peace, he advised his Friends not to oppose it in its Progress, *but find fault with it after it was made:* Which would be a Copy of the like Usage themselves had met with after the Treaty of Riswick; and *the safest, as well as the most probable way* of disgracing the Promoters and Advisers."

1. C. L. Stevenson, *Ethics and Language* (New Haven, Yale University Press, 1944), p. 278. In spite of differences, I am greatly indebted throughout this chapter to Stevenson's treatment of "persuasive definitions."

metal," and the assertion, clearly enough, is that "imaginative sensitivity and originality" resemble "culture" but are actually different from it in important respects. The descriptive meaning of culture is restricted to the *appearance* of what is generally recognized as culture. This kind of redefinition may be rendered plausible by our recognizing the presence of certain virtues in men who do not possess other qualities which we include in the idea of culture. It will be fully acceptable only to a person who considers these virtues as more valuable than the remaining elements of culture, e.g., acquired knowledge, restraint, or technical skill. In any case we must recognize that there is a shift not simply in "emotive meaning" but in meaning of a descriptive sort as well, however vague. The task of rhetoric would not be very interesting if it could perform verbal magic by transferring emotive force. It is the readjustment of all elements of meaning to a new rhetorical end that gives the task complexity and makes rhetoric an art.

We have seen Swift discredit completely such terms as "persecution" and "common enemy" as they are used by the dissenters. In other cases, we can see him performing more patient redefinition. He can extend the meaning of "pedantry," for example, so as to acquit men of learning of a unique vice and also to make clear the equivalence of other unnamed vices:

> pedantry is the too frequent or unseasonable obtruding our own knowledge in common discourse, and placing too great a value upon it; by which definition, men of the court or the army may be as guilty of pedantry as a philosopher or a divine; and, it is the same vice in women, when they are over copious upon the subject of their petticoats, or their fans, or their china.[2]

This has the charm of turning the easiest complaint of light-brained people against themselves. But even more it is, like any metaphor, a new kind of classification; the "pedantry of fans" is, like Thomas Habington's phrase, the "rhetoric of clothes," a new way of regarding behavior. Any definition is such a way of regarding something anew, a provisional classification. Neologisms and metaphors are means of naming new classifications. But only the neologism is free from the funded meaning of terms; the metaphor, or the "persuasive definition" we find in Swift, carries along the valuative meaning of its words largely unchanged but gives that valuation a new basis. Ladies discussing china are seen under the aspect of Martinus Scriblerus or Smollett's Dr. Wagtail; the new class to be named by "pedantry" has a wider membership but with very similar qualifications. Swift has, in Stevenson's words, given a term

2. *Hints towards an Essay on Conversation*, TS, xi, 70. See a similar passage in *A Treatise on Good Manners and Good Breeding*, TS, xi, 81–2.

"greater precision within the bounds of its customary vagueness." [3] The new precision is one of specifying a motive, and it sacrifices in turn the precision of limiting the term to affectation of learning in the conventional sense. Yet the simplicity of seeing all this behavior as pedantry and as comparable in motive makes the novel use of the term satisfying both as discovery and as economy and distracts us from the losses suffered.

In another instance, from a letter Swift wrote to a friend, we can see an attempt to divorce the idea of "bravery"—and its favorable valuative force—from display of courage, by making modesty an attribute:

> there is nothing I have greater contempt for than what is usually styled bravery, which really consists in never giving just offence, and yet by a general demeanour makes it appear that we do not want courage, though our hand is not every hour at our hilt. [4]

The use of "really" is a good symptom of the persuasive definition. Here the descriptive meaning is revised to exclude the bully and braggart, however genuine their courage. By limiting the range of those to be considered "brave," the definition changes the meaning of the term; but the use of "really" asserts the conformity of this meaning of "bravery" with the usual favorable sense of the term. Here again we have a selection of some part of the usual range of meaning of the term and an exclusion of another part, with the effect of redefining the word and changing its applicability without changing in any marked way its valuative direction.

REDEFINITION AND OTHER METHODS

In the cases of "persecution" and "common enemy" we find Swift dismissing a valuative term by exposing its vagueness and turning that vagueness into a characterization of those who use it. In the case of "pedantry" he extends the usual reference of a strongly valuative term; in the case of "bravery" he restricts it. In all these instances the act of definition serves to redirect attitudes. The obtrusiveness with which Swift exploits the vagueness or the ambiguity of terms varies with his tone and the end of a specific work. At times the process of redefinition is kept implicit. It is realized by a gradual shift of terms such as hardly arouses awareness of the direction it is taking until it has made possible explicit and forceful antithesis. The opening of *The Sentiments of a Church of England Man* provides a good illustration:

3. Stevenson, *Ethics and Language*, p. 210.
4. *Correspondence*, III, 81 (Swift to Knightley Chetwode, 9 May 1721).

Whoever hath examined the Conduct and Proceedings of both Parties for some years past, whether in or out of Power, cannot well conceive it possible to go far towards the Extreams of either, without offering some Violence to his Integrity or Understanding. A wise and a good Man may indeed be sometimes induced to comply with a Number, whose Opinion he generally approves, although it be perhaps against his own. But this Liberty should be made use of upon very few Occasions, and those of small Importance, and then only with a View of bringing over his own Side another Time to something of greater and more publick Moment. But, to sacrifice the Innocency of a friend, the Good of our Country, or our own Conscience to the Humour, or Passion, or Interest of a Party; plainly shews that either our heads or our hearts are not as they should be: Yet this very Practice is the fundamental Law of each Faction among us; as may be obvious to any who will impartially, and without Engagement, be at the Pains to examine their Actions.[5]

In this passage the variation of epithets provides implicit redefinition. The first sentence is deliberate and judicious, but each of its careful qualifications makes its meaning exhaustive. The phrase "some Violence" is typical: perhaps not much violence but in no case none at all. The concluding words "Integrity or Understanding" are immediately taken up in the next sentence by "a wise and a good Man." Such a man may be "induced to comply"; the terms are at best reluctantly concessive. In the third sentence the variation becomes more striking; compliance becomes a "Liberty" whose exercise is to be carefully limited. The failure to limit it is expanded in a series of offenses; the "Number, whose Opinion he generally approves," is transformed into "the Humour, or Passion, or Interest of a Party," and those who commit such liberties (presumably against integrity and understanding) are in the clearest terms not wise and good—their heads or hearts are "not as they should be." And just as the moral criticism of partisanship becomes most explicit and vigorous, the demands of party are stated most forcibly, for "this very Practice" is "the fundamental Law" of faction—a law which, by implication, is opposed to moral law. Thus in a few sentences Swift has gradually intensified the meaning of party loyalty by setting it against the canons of morality. By varying predications until he can establish the valuative meaning of his terms, he has transformed a scruple into indignant censure.

What Swift does here we have already seen him do in the sermons. By means of variation, he constantly redefines his terms so as to make valuative meanings more readily accessible. The terms retain a common denotation, but they give us a progressively stronger judgment of what

5. *The Sentiments of a Church of England Man with Respect to Religion and Government*, HD, II, 1 (TS, III, 51).

they denote. By placing an object in a new context where new relations become evident, redefinition provides the ground for revaluation. The plain style simply changes the terms of its argument without calling attention to what it is doing. It is, actually, achieving in a new manner much the same end as the metaphysical style before it or as Swift's own more conspicuously witty style. And it has the sudden surprise of wit when the results of the unobtrusive process are stated in the bold conclusion.

If redefinition is a technique for placing a term in a new context, we can also see the context being prepared to make a persuasive definition acceptable. This is pre-eminently the method of Swift's symbolic satires, where the practical judgments follow, as it were, deductively from the system he has created. Systems confirm novel definitions by giving them a place in a coherent pattern, by making them inevitable if the pattern is to maintain its coherence. We can see this device at work in Swift's earliest political tract, *The Contests and Dissensions . . . in Athens and Rome* (1701). Swift was writing to defend the Whig lords who had been impeached by the Commons for their part in the Partition Treaties. His task, like that of other Whig writers, was to make the action of Commons seem as much a case of tyranny as the act of any simple despot. Swift alone made effective use of the theory of the mixed state to give "Tyranny" a new and applicable definition.

The doctrine of the mixed state had gained great currency in the seventeenth century. Men like Temple and Swift, who refused to speculate about a contractual or patriarchal origin of the state, found in the balance of powers a historical tradition to be cultivated. The state, it was held, consisted of the One, the Few, and the Many. If any of these elements held all the power, the result would be one of the classical forms of pure government. The pure forms, however, succeeded each other in an endless cycle which could only be broken by the establishment of a balance of all powers, and for Swift's age the balance was established by the constitution. If the mixed state could not achieve immortality through perfect balance, as some had hoped, it could at least maintain its health for a long time, like a man whose body enjoyed a balance of humors.[6] The chief danger to the state, then, was destruction of the balance, and tyranny could be ascribed to whichever power might destroy it:

> When the Ballance is broke . . . the Power will never continue long in equal Division between the two remaining Parties, but (until the ballance is fixed anew) will run entirely into one. This gives the truest

6. For a full study of the theory of the mixed state, see Zera Fink, *The Classical Republicans: An Essay in the Recovery of a Pattern of Thought in Seventeenth Century England* (Evanston, Northwestern University Press, 1945). For a contrast to Swift's pamphlet, see John Lord Somers, *Jura Populi Anglicani: or, the Subject's Right of Petitioning Set Forth* (London, 1701), esp. pp. 17–29.

Account of what is understood in the most ancient and approved *Greek*
Authors, by the word *Tyranny;* which is not meant for the seizing
of the uncontrouled, or absolute Power into the hands of a single Person; (as many superficial Men have grosly mistaken) but for the breaking of the Ballance by whatever Hand, and leaving the Power wholly
in one scale. For *Tyranny* and *Usurpation* in a State, are by no Means
confined to any Number.

Swift has carefully prepared his reader for the new definition of tyranny.
But he does more. He goes on to show that the tyranny of the many must
end in the tyranny of a single person, that the Commons who break the
balance "will be sure to run upon the very Rock, that they meant to
avoid." This has the virtue of making the new definition accord with the
old, and it also provides an opening for the satiric device we shall see
again in *The Conduct of the Allies*—the image of the dupe accomplishing
all that he most wishes to prevent.

Now, we have shewn, that although most Revolutions of Government
in *Greece* and *Rome* began with the Tyranny of the People, yet they
generally concluded in that of a single Person. So that a usurping
Populace is its own *Dupe;* a meer Underworker, and a Purchaser in
Trust for some single Tyrant; whose State and Power they advance
to their own Ruin, with as blind an Instinct as those Worms that die
with weaving magnificent Habits for Beings of a superior Nature to
their own.[7]

The force of this passage comes from the surprise of the metaphor. As
an image of blind instinct, it serves aptly enough, as do the "magnificent
Habits" for political power. But the metaphor allows Swift to accomplish
more; in providing the contrast between the lowly silkworm and the
"superior" man, it enables him to emphasize the yielding of manhood with
power. The people and the tyrant are beings of the same nature. Only
the gullibility of the people can exalt a tyrant, and only their abject surrender of power can reduce them to worms.

The Contests and Dissensions, then, starts with the symbolic framework of the balanced state, basing upon it a redefinition of tyranny. This
redefinition allows Swift to reduce what might seem greater liberty of
the people into potential tyranny and ultimate destruction of all liberty.
Once his own definition is clearly set forth, he can attack in turn the vagueness of his opponents' terms. For Swift believes that "in order to preserve the Ballance in a mixed State, the Limits of Power deposited with
each Party ought to be ascertained, and generally known." The failure to
set such limits is developed in two figures which convert the vagueness of
terms, as in the use of the dissenters, into potential disaster:

7. HD, I, 197–8, 227 (TS, I, 233, 262).

But to fix one Foot of their Compass wherever they think fit, and extend the other to such terrible Lengths, without describing any Circumference at all; is to leave us, and themselves, in a very uncertain
State, and in a Sort of *Rotation,* that the Author of the *Oceana* never
dreamt of . . . How far must we proceed, or where shall we stop?
The *Raging of the Sea,* and *the Madness of the People,* are put together
in Holy Writ; and it is God, alone, who can say to either, *Hitherto shalt
thou pass, and no farther.*[8]

The first figure is much like the reductive definition of "persecution,"
here dramatized in the operation of a compass. The failure to describe
a circumference is the very negation of the function of a compass. The
second figure, enforced by its allusion to Scripture, considers power once
limits are impossible. The "terrible Lengths" of the compass are transformed into the limitless sea. The image of sea admits the idea of turbulence, and turbulence readily becomes the "Madness of the People."
Thus the slight logical matrix of compass, limitlessness, rotation, Oceana,
raging sea, madness of the people permits Swift by shifts of terms to turn
the folly of uncompassed power into the terror of an uncontrollable popular fury.

In *The Contests and Dissensions* redefinition is both end and means;
it grows out of and leads back into a symbolic framework. This is often
the case in Swift. Redefinition is not, as a rule, so explicit as in most
of the cases examined here; rather, it is implied in shifts of terms, whether
the unobtrusive shifts of the plain style or the extravagant reversals of wit.
It is central, however, to Swift's rhetorical purpose and a key to his conception of a rational appeal. The way in which men use words not only
expresses their attitudes but often serves to shape them. Words bring
the weight of traditional sentiments to bear upon the present, and it is a
necessary task to make their misapplication clear without seeking to overthrow the sentiments themselves. Swift's appeal is not to throw off these
sentiments as mere prejudices but rather to correct the intellectual error
which would invoke them improperly.

"THE MERE WEIGHT OF FACTS"

It may be useful at this point to turn to a work notable as an example
of Swift's plain style. Johnson, for example, felt that *The Conduct of the
Allies* "operates by the mere weight of facts, with very little assistance
from the hand that produced them." [9] More recent critics have not agreed

8. HD, I, 200–1, 231 (TS, I, 236, 265).

9. Samuel Johnson, *Lives of the Poets,* ed. G. B. Hill (Oxford, Clarendon Press,
1905), p. 19, para. 48. See Wimsatt, *Prose Style of Johnson,* pp. 98–9, for a collection of
Johnson's comments on Swift's style.

about the source of the pamphlet's effect. Henry Craik attributed its power to the "unrelenting indignation with which it is inspired." Winston Churchill has described it as a "cool and massive catalogue" of the short-comings of the allies.[1] There need be no contradiction between these views if one sees how the indignation is expressed through an apparently detached, satiric view. For Swift claims simply to uncover truth rather than to awaken passions, and his manner is the typical one of the ex-aminer, skeptically testing assertions by empirical evidence, soberly ap-plying reasonable principles to the case in question. Only at intervals does he allow himself to voice a judgment, and it is often a judgment offered not as his own but as that of a posterity freed of local loyalties and tem-porary blindness:

> Posterity will be at a loss to conceive what kind of Spirit could possess their Ancestors, who after ten Years Suffering, by the unexampled Politicks of a Nation, maintaining a War by annually Pawning it self; and during a short Peace, while they were looking back with Horrour on the heavy Load of Debts they had contracted; universally con-demning those pernicious Counsels which had occasioned them; rack-ing their Invention for some Remedies or Expedients to mend their shattered Condition: That these very People, without giving them-selves time to breathe, should again enter into a more dangerous, chargeable, and extensive War, for the same, or perhaps a greater Period of Time, and without any apparent Necessity.[2]

This passage leaves no doubt about rhetorical ordering—in the cumula-tive effect of the participial phrases, the contrast of a long war and a short peace, and the latent imagery of desperation and recklessness. Such passages as this are, however, exceptional in the earlier parts of the pamphlet. For each explicit summary and ordering, there is a much longer recitation of facts, what Johnson considered counting.

"Swift has told what he had to tell distinctly enough, but that is all. He had to count ten, and he has counted it right." [3] To meet Johnson's criticism, one must look behind the façade of counting, for, although Swift professes only to reveal true facts, his artlessness is part of the deliberately assumed ethos of the examiner. *The Conduct of the Allies* was written at a time when the war had ceased to be widely popular but when the reasons for giving it up, particularly without a "hard" peace, could only appear narrowly prudential beside the patriotic zeal

1. *Swift: Selections from His Works,* ed. Henry Craik (Oxford, Clarendon Press, 1892), I, 20–1. Winston S. Churchill, *Marlborough: His Life and Times* (New York, Scribner's, 1938), VI, 506.
2. HD, VI, 18–19 (TS, V, 75).
3. James Boswell, *Life of Johnson,* ed. G. B. Hill and L. F. Powell (Oxford, Clar-endon Press, 1934), II, 65. See above, p. 31 n. 9.

of its proponents. "It seems incredible," Marlborough's chaplain had preached,

> that Men should, for many Years together, struggle with the greatest
> Difficulties, and successfully go through innumerable Dangers, in
> pursuit of a noble End, an End worthy of all the Pains and Troubles
> they are at; and yet lose their Courage as they gain Ground, and shame-
> fully give out just at last, without Spirit, and dead-hearted; when the
> glorious End they have so long aimed at, is in sight, and almost in their
> Possession.[4]

Swift's task was to dissociate true patriotism from military glory and to strip the war of its nobility.

Swift lays the grounds for this revaluation carefully. He opens the tract with a brief statement of principles which are admirably simple and reasonable but which carry the germs of the more striking simplifica-tions that follow. No monarch will engage in any but a defensive war "beyond a certain degree," lest the nation become so weakened that it cannot survive even a victory:

> this would be to run into real infallible Ruin, only in hopes to remove
> what might perhaps but appear so by a probable Speculation.

The balance of this sentence is weighted deliberately: simple certainties are offset by elaborately hedged possibilities. It is this contrast which runs through the tract: real against apparent interest, prudence against illu-sion.

From this point on, the dissociation of war from prudence and honor becomes progressively sharper. In the second paragraph, Swift sets forth the conditions under which a prince may undertake war. Without a strong, unified, and prosperous people, "he will hardly be persuaded to disturb the World's Quiet and his own, while there is any other way left of preserving the latter with Honour and Safety." War has been reduced by careful abstraction to that which violates "Quiet," and "Quiet" carries enough suggestion of peace and sobriety to leave war little import but offensive disorder. Among the attributes Swift strips away is "Glory": "our Victories were then of some Use as well as Glory; for we were so prudent to Fight, and so happy to Conquer, only for our selves." [5] Here the parallelism of "prudent" and "happy" turns upon the usefulness of war and leaves "Glory" without meaning at all. The same technique finally produces an ironic dismissal of another honorific term, "Valour":

4. "The Charge of God to Joshua," a Thanksgiving sermon delivered before the duke of Marlborough, 9 September 1711, after the victory of Bouchain, *The Works of the Late Right Reverend and Learned Dr. Francis Hare, Lord Bishop of Chichester* (London, 1746), I, 64. For a reply to this sermon, see *A Learned Comment upon Dr. Hare's Excellent Sermon*, TS, v, 169–85, probably the work of Mrs. Manley with Swift's as-sistance.

5. HD, VI, 7, 8, 10 (TS, v, 63, 64, 65).

We are destroying many thousand Lives, exhausting all our Substance, not for our own Interest, which would be but common Prudence; not for a Thing indifferent, which would be sufficient Folly, but perhaps to our own Destruction, which is perfect Madness. We may live to feel the Effects of our Valour more sensibly than all the Consequences we imagine from the Dominions of *Spain* in the Duke of *Anjou*.[6]

With this preparation, Swift's specific criticism gains point. The war served the interest of England's allies, although it cost England greater "Blood and Treasure." It could, moreover, only be supported by men who have a private interest since the nation gains nothing. As the war led more and more clearly to England's destruction, it became a sacrifice of the nation to the interest of the few, and the few were epitomized by the avaricious and vainglorious Marlborough.

In presenting these facts, Swift assumes a detachment which leads inevitably to a satiric view of England furiously battling for her own defeat. The incongruities of her position suggest an almost mechanical folly, which Swift intensifies by stressing the imperious parasitism of the allies:

This kind of treatment from our two Principal Allies, hath taught the same Dialect to all the rest; so that there is hardly a petty Prince, whom we half maintain by Subsidies and Pensions, who is not ready, upon every Occasion, to threaten Us, that He will recall His Troops (though they must rob or starve at home) if we refuse to comply with Him in any Demand, however so unreasonable.[7]

The conduct of the allies is made the responsibility of the English people. It was "our blind Zeal for pushing on the War at all Adventures" that encouraged the Austrian emperor to default; he had only to present a gift to Marlborough and then "wisely [leave] us to fight [his] Battles." The reception of the English envoy to the Dutch was "such a one, as those only deserve, who are content to take." In helping the Dutch to free Flanders from the French, Marlborough has allowed them to set up a greater tyranny than any he has overthrown. All these evils arise from a commitment to a war whose end is forgotten or rather made unattainable by the insistence on "no peace without Spain." The English have no clear interest to pursue and thus no way of determining when their ends have been achieved. They have become "the *Dupes* and *Bubbles* of Europe"—and, even more, of a native group of *"Monied Men,"* "whose perpetual Harvest is War, and whose beneficial way of Traffick must very much decline by a Peace." The allies have accordingly revised their own war aims, pushing their own interest at the expense of their "dupes," as the Barrier Treaty has made clear:

6. HD, vi, 20 (TS, v, 77).
7. HD, vi, 24 (TS, v, 81).

By this Treaty, the Condition of the War, with respect to the *Dutch,* was widely altered: They fought no longer for Security, but for Grandeur; and we, instead of labouring to make them *safe,* must beggar ourselves to render them *Formidable.*[8]

It is for sentences like this that the array of facts prepares; here the satiric reversal is fully exposed in the double antithesis of Dutch ends and English means and in the ominous overtones which are released by the final contrast of "safe" and "Formidable." Swift can see allies not only as present accomplices but as future rivals. The misused effort to rectify one balance is the force that overturns another.

Perhaps the most striking paragraph in the tract is one which looks back upon the war from the point of view of a posterity committed by public credit to pay for it:

It will, no doubt, be a mighty Comfort to our Grandchildren, when they see a few Rags hang up in *Westminster-Hall,* which cost an hundred Millions, whereof they are paying the Arrears, and boasting, as Beggars do, that their Grandfathers were Rich and Great.[9]

The reduction of war is complete, abstracted from the glories of Marlborough's victories, seen with the detachment of time, its trophies turned to "Rags." The cant of beggars is the only praise which reason can allow defrauded heirs to yield. This is the kind of simplification that is Swift's special gift. Whatever judgment one makes of the soundness of his view, one must recognize that Swift is doing more than "counting ten." The whole tract is carefully framed to convert the claims of glory to folly, and Swift has directed all his evidence to expose not only the aimlessness of English policy but also the sheer destruction which its apparent triumphs achieved. This framework is a typical satiric one; we find it earlier in *A Tale of a Tub,* where the very claims to renown of the moderns are a guarantee of their oblivion. We can see it in *Don Quixote* or *Hudibras* as well, in Pope's *Dunciad,* even in Milton's treatment of Pandemonium. But a "cool perusal" such as Johnson claims should give attention to this rhetorical framework as well as to the factual evidence which is fitted into it. The facts may have been the striking novelty in 1711 and may have given the framework its justification; but the same facts might well have been turned to quite different effect. Only when we accept the rhetorical function of the tract as well as the informative do such passages as this last seem more than added color or ornament. The proper words become precise and often metaphorical, the proper places become elaborately antithetical, when they make emphatic the significance Swift has been implying throughout.

8. HD, vi, 34, 32, 40, 41, 49 (TS, v, 91, 89, 97, 99, 106).
9. HD, vi, 55–6 (TS, v, 113).

III

The Method of Wit

True and False Wit

THE destruction which Swift performs as examiner clears the ground for the new structures he builds as satirist. But more than this, the two processes become one: the very act of destruction is only a reshaping of materials for their use in a radically new structure. For wit, as Freud has said, "goes to the trouble of searching for the word which comprises both ideas. Indeed, it must often at first transform the expression of one of the ideas into an unusual form until it furnishes an associative connection with the second thought." [1] We can make a distinction here between the kind of transformation which is not obvious—the gradual reordering of the context of the word—and the kind which frankly uses the ambiguity of a word to move, as through a looking glass, into a new context. The first of these we have seen in the method of redefinition and, in fact, throughout Swift's plain style; the second is more conspicuously verbal, at once more striking and more extravagant. It begins with a violation of logic and justifies that violation by an implicit logic on a deeper level. Only by destroying the strict order of meanings can it invoke a more important meaning; its disrespect for words is a demand for a radical reinterpretation.

Except for puns, which are useful but limited, metaphors are perhaps the best source of such witty ambiguities. For metaphor is always implicit analogy, but the basis of the analogy—the common qualities of the objects metaphor relates—is left "open," to be determined by inference. [2] The variety of points of analogy gives, first of all, a depth of awareness that has led one critic to call metaphor a "stereoscope of ideas." [3] In considering the possible points of analogy which may be relevant in a metaphor, we try to see in both objects all qualities they may possibly have

1. Sigmund Freud, *Wit and Its Relation to the Unconscious,* in *The Basic Writings,* ed. and tr. A. A. Brill (New York, Modern Library, 1938), p. 655.
2. See the discussion of "open simile" and "metaphor" in Monroe C. Beardsley, *Straight Thinking: A Guide for Readers & Writers* (New York, Prentice-Hall, 1950), pp. 96–104.
3. William B. Stanford, *Greek Metaphor: Studies in Theories and Practice* (Oxford, Blackwell, 1936), p. 105: "By presenting two different points of view in one idea, that is by approaching the word through two different meanings, it gives the illusion and conviction of solidity and reality. Thus metaphor adds a new dimension to language as a vehicle of imagination and thought."

in common. (This fullness of attention is often taken as distinctively aesthetic, as an awareness of the "world's body.") Second, the metaphor allows a number of possible interpretations, each of which requires an alternate paraphrase and each of which may be extended by the writer at will. Metaphor is a fertile source of wit precisely because it implies many bases for analogy. It abstracts common properties from both objects—from tenor and vehicle—and gives them a name, but the name is applicable to any of these properties or to all.

The metaphor, then, can become highly ambiguous, and its ambiguity was nowhere more fully exploited than in the poetry of the metaphysicals. Rosemond Tuve has most fully treated the conceit as "an image based simultaneously on a number of predicaments or common places of logic" and has shown its logical complexity in the witty poets.[4] The use of the conceit in conspicuously syllogistic poetry made for striking conclusions but also for evident sophistry. The sophistry is of small concern when it is used not to prove a point but rather to assert it with ingenious hyperbole and when its use is a convention whose reception is appropriate.

We can see in the metaphysical conceit the spirit which honors God—or the mistress, seen as divine—with an extravagance which can never be extravagant enough. If logic is flouted, the conclusions are none the less sound and all the more a cause for wonder. There is, moreover, something of the lavish use of gifts that Ruskin recognized in Gothic ornament—the desire to turn all one's powers to the act of celebration. When Andrewes shows that the very syntax of a scriptural passage points to his conclusion, he is not resting his case upon such adventitious evidence. Rather the conclusion is itself so persuasive, on other grounds, that one can find testimony for it everywhere. The certainty and satisfaction one feels in the conclusion demand more than simply rational evidence as their basis. One can see the counterpart of this in the desire to order each element of the universe and each of the arts, as Boethius and Augustine did music, into part of a pattern seen throughout. We can see it again in Herbert's shaped poems or in the "wreathèd garland" he weaves in verse to furnish "a crown of praise." Finally one must recognize the deliberate cultivation of surprise in the turning of the most unlikely objects to an inevitable purpose. All these ends are achieved by the careful distortion of which Freud speaks. Nothing is quite as we might expect it to be; it contains the germs of something quite different. The technique of introducing a term with one emphasis and developing it with another makes the apparently irrelevant suggestion leap suddenly to attention and assert its primacy.

However one may admire the sensibility which finds expression in

4. Rosemond Tuve, *Elizabethan and Metaphysical Imagery: Renaissance Poetic and Twentieth Century Critics* (Chicago, University of Chicago Press, 1947), p. 264; see also pp. 344-5, 355.

metaphysical wit, one can see the dangers in either too literal a reception or too frivolous a use of it. In an age seeking agreements the verbal
ingenuities of wit seemed an opening for unlimited idiosyncrasy and
insoluble dispute. The manner of the metaphysicals, moreover, had
turned into literary mannerism for many poets; without the strength
of impulse which an earlier piety had given it, it could seem as specious
and lifeless as the noble Victorian abstractions seemed in the twenties
of this century.[5] In the Augustan attempt to "found a new Good City on
the basis of sound reason, common sense, and good taste," [6] a new stability was sought in language, a clear relation of words to things. We
have seen this reaction become a demand for stricter definition. In the
prose controversies of the Restoration, meanwhile, wit became largely
a destructive rhetorical instrument, partly parody, partly bantering reduction of opponents' terms.

One writer in particular seems to underlie the decline of both the
rhetorical and the poetic conceit from their original seriousness. Samuel
Butler, in *Hudibras*, turned the conceit into a brilliant burlesque device.
Charles Cotton had debased the epic style of Virgil in his *Scarronides*
and had made constant use of bathos, but he did not parody the metaphysical style. Butler, on the other hand, in his antipathy toward tenuous
speculation, his hatred of enthusiasm, and his contempt for the tortured
wit of Benlowes, found in the wit of the metaphysicals the very idiom
of the forced logic of hypocrite or dupe.[7] The incongruous conceit, which
at its best transcended logic, became in Butler a form of debasing analogy,
which returned as insistently to the physical and mechanical as had the
earlier conceit to the divine and suprahuman. The effect was a thorough
inversion: the transcendence of reason became an incapacity for it, and
the pious hyperboles became frenetic ingenuities of rationalization. Swift
in his "Ode to Dr. William Sancroft" expresses very well the attitude
Butler's method suggested:

> *And some, to be large cyphers in a state,*
> *Pleas'd with an empty swelling to be counted great;*
> *Make their minds travel o'er infinity of space,*

5. Cf. Stephen Spender, *World within World* (New York, Harcourt, Brace, 1951),
p. 7: "Just as Midas turned everything he touched to gold, so my father turned everything into rhetorical abstraction, in which there was no concreteness, no accuracy. . . . A
game of football ceased to be just the kicking about of a leather ball by bare-kneed boys.
It had become confused with the Battle of Life. Honor, Integrity, Discipline, Toughness
and a dozen other qualities haunted the field like ghostly footballers."
6. W. H. Auden, *The Enchafèd Flood* (New York, Random House, 1950), p. 50.
7. Cf. *Minor Poets of the Caroline Period*, ed. George Saintsbury (Oxford, Clarendon Press, 1921), I, 311: Butler's "own method is often only that of Benlowes changed
from unconscious indulgence to conscious and deliberate utilization for comic effect."
For an important discussion of the philosophic grounds for Butler's art, see Ricardo
Quintana, "Samuel Butler: A Restoration Figure in a Modern Light," *ELH, 18* (1951),
7–31.

Rapp'd through the wide expanse of thought,
And oft in contradiction's vortex caught,
To keep that worthless clod, the body, in one place.[8]

The shift from "false" to "true" wit is radical yet not so radical as the Augustan adjectives might suggest. George Williamson has traced it as a movement to "a new style of wit which depended less upon the ambiguity than upon the antithesis of ideas, or less upon the startling reconciliations and more upon surprising oppositions." [9] If we take the shift as a movement from the startling to the surprising, we are at least saved from reading the Augustan terms in too narrow a sense. Augustan "true wit" is a wedding of fancy and judgment. It is true to taste in sacrificing the irrelevant and the irregular for the sake of a stricter propriety. The plain prose style of Swift is one illustration of this new kind of propriety, a closeness of design that supports a richness of suggestion without surrendering to it. "True wit" was also regarded as being in some sense true to fact; for Addison true wit depended upon a resemblance of ideas rather than mere words. It resists extravagance and hyperbole and limits itself to comparatively few and fairly conventional metaphors. There is the counterpart of metaphor in such devices as antithesis; and, as we have seen, metaphor and antithesis are constantly played off against each other as Swift moves between abstract diction and the abstraction of metaphor. Yet if true wit does not parade its rejection of strict reasoning and literal assertion, it certainly evades their limits. Addison recognized that true wit to be wit at all must surprise us, and this surprise is scarcely to be obtained without verbal play. If one takes "true" in the sense of fidelity to literal fact, true wit is a self-contradictory phrase.[1] We can, however, better examine this shift from false to true wit—and the underlying continuity—in two familiar and somewhat similar passages, the "canonizations" of Donne's lovers and Pope's unfortunate lady:

We can dye by it, if not live by love,
And if unfit for tombes and hearse
Our legend bee, it will be fit for verse;
And if no peece of Chronicle wee prove,

8. *Poems,* 1, 36, lines 59–64.
9. George Williamson, "The Rhetorical Pattern of Neo-Classical Wit," *Modern Philology, 33* (1935), 74–5.
1. In *Spectator,* No. 62 (11 May 1711), Addison distinguishes true, false, and mixed wit: "As *true Wit* consists in the Resemblance of Ideas, and *false Wit* in the Resemblance of Words . . . there is another kind of Wit which consists partly in the Resemblance of Ideas, and partly in the Resemblance of Words; which for Distinction Sake I shall call *mixt Wit.*" Addison confuses the problem by citing Locke's epistemological distinction (between wit and reason or judgment) and thus giving to "true" the rather narrow sense of literal truth. In these terms, there is clearly no wit at all of artistic value but "mixt Wit." I have used the terms "true wit" and "false wit" loosely to indicate two extremes of what is properly "mixt Wit."

> We'll build in sonnets pretty roomes;
> As well a well wrought urne becomes
> The greatest ashes, as halfe-acre tombes,
> And by these hymnes, all shall approve
> Us Canoniz'd for Love.

For Donne, the contrast of the world's values and the lovers' is worked out in the opposition of tombs and verse, an opposition which is pursued through the following lines in the imagery of building. The "peece of Chronicle" is offset by "sonnets pretty roomes"; this suggests the contrast of worldly dignity and diminutive artfulness. The "sonnets pretty roomes" are taken up again in the "well wrought urne," which carries over the meanings of size and artifice but acquires in addition the sense of something pure and appropriate, the intense realization in a small space of what is clumsily achieved in "halfe-acre tombes." Thus the introduction of "halfe-acre tombes" marks the clearest turning of the scale of values; here the world's dignities acquire a specious heaviness, and by contrast the lovers' achievements lose their suggestion of triviality and become decorous. The shift from diminutive artfulness to compact and pure art is now extended (in a return to the imagery of verse) to the purity of devotion of "hymnes" and finally to the pure devotion itself of canonization. One may complain that this is sophistical, that the triviality of the "pretty roomes" is not the artistry of a "well wrought urne," that the dignity of the chronicles is not so invidious as the ostentation of the tombs. But Donne plays upon the ambiguity of his terms in order to move through two parallel links of analogies until normal values are completely reversed.

> What tho' no weeping Loves thy ashes grace,
> Nor polish'd marble emulate thy face?
> What tho' no sacred earth allow thee room,
> Nor hallow'd dirge be mutter'd o'er thy tomb?
> Yet shall thy grave with rising flow'rs be drest,
> And the green turf lie lightly on thy breast:
> There shall the morn her earliest tears bestow,
> There the first roses of the year shall blow;
> While Angels with their silver wings o'ershade
> The ground, now sacred by thy reliques made.[2]

Pope's lines set up a similar opposition, but in a manner less conspicuously paradoxical. The worldly dignities are stated in the first four lines. These are denied the lady. With the pivotal "yet," Pope invokes the consolations of Nature (with all its implied superiority to Man). The images of rising life are opposed to falling grief; the coldness of statuary

---

2. John Donne, "The Canonization," lines 28–36; Alexander Pope, "Elegy to the Memory of an Unfortunate Lady," lines 59–68. Cf. Cleanth Brooks, *The Well Wrought Urn* (New York, Reynal and Hitchcock, 1947), pp. 10–17.

"Loves" and "polish'd marble" is opposed to the "morn." The images of natural beauty—vivid and lively even in grief—overshadow the worldly honors so completely that we are prepared for the apotheosis in the last couplet. The natural loveliness is readily transformed into angelic protection, the ashes into a saint's "reliques." Both poets work through the opposition of two sets of images. Donne seems only to argue, Pope only to describe, yet both use images as arguments as well as symbols. Donne surprises with sudden shifts of meaning until his symbols have emerged; Pope gradually discloses the symbolic weight of his descriptive terms until an argument has been implied. Pope does not need the dialectical cleverness of false wit. His lines are less difficult but also less intense; he is restricted to more conventional symbols because he can only suggest them. There are losses as well as gains in each method; what matters here is a recognition of both similarity and difference.

The true wit of the Augustan poet has more in common with the method of Swift's plain prose than these lines from Pope can show, for they lack the sharpness of parallel and antithesis which marks the couplet at its best. Whatever else it accomplishes, the form of the couplet serves to express, in its surprising oppositions, the careful discrimination of the sound from the specious:

> In vain thy Reason finer webs shall draw,
> Entangle Justice in her net of Law,
> And right, too rigid, harden into wrong;
> Still for the strong too weak, the weak too strong.

This sense of imminent corruption, of right hardening into wrong, imposes a task on the poet similar to Swift's technique of redefinition. Even more, the couplet serves the Augustan effort to fix the undefinable norm as the poise of opposed abstractions or generalities, each in itself too rigid to provide a workable standard:

> Careless of censure, nor too fond of fame;
> Still pleased to praise, yet not afraid to blame,
> Averse alike to flatter, or offend;
> Not free from faults, nor yet too vain to mend.

So John Pomfret in his description of "some Obliging, Modest Fair" stresses the flexibility of a consistent decorum:

> I'd have her Reason all her Passions sway;
> Easy in Company, in Private Gay:
> Coy to a Fop, to the Deserving Free,
> Still Constant to her self, and Just to me.

Or Addison, the paradox of shifting propriety in the show of courage:

> Lodg'd in the soul, with virtue over-rul'd,
> Inflam'd by reason, and by reason cool'd,

> *In hours of peace content to be unknown,*
> *And only in the field of battel shown.*[3]

Again, in Swift's poem *To Mrs. Biddy Floyd,* we can see the same discriminations worked out but in contrasting couplets rather than within the line:

> *When* Cupid *did his Grandsire* Jove *intreat,*
> *To form some Beauty by a new Receit,*
> Jove *sent and found far in a Country Scene,*
> *Truth, Innocence, Good Nature, Look serene;*
> *From which Ingredients, First the dext'rous Boy*
> *Pickt the Demure, the Aukward, and the Coy;*
> *The* Graces *from the Court did next provide*
> *Breeding and Wit, and Air, and decent Pride;*
> *These* Venus *cleans'd from ev'ry spurious Grain*
> *Of Nice, Coquet, Affected, Pert, and Vain.*
> Jove *mix'd up all, and his best Clay imploy'd;*
> *Then call'd the happy Composition,* Floyd.[4]

True wit such as this constantly exposes the ambiguity of terms and checks right from hardening into wrong. It gains its freshness by making the complexity of terms evident, by pointing up their conflicting implications. False wit does not expose this ambiguity so much as exploit it. Its frank sophistry disclaims the responsibility of strict persuasion, and once freed it can admit shifts of meaning and tenuous extension of metaphor. It seeks those terms, in fact, whose ambiguity is potentially greatest; hence its fondness for metaphor and concrete analogy. False wit serves, therefore, as an expansion of a tendency always present in true wit. For Swift, it often provides the culmination of an apparently plain passage whose slight shifts of terms have prepared for the final witty overstatement.

Swift's work begins in the high style of wit, or as much as survived in Cowley, but it moves in two parallel paths, toward the satiric use of debased false wit on the one hand and toward the propriety of true wit in a style that becomes increasingly ironic. Swift was once told, he reported, "that my mind was like a conjured spirit, that would do mischief if I would not give it employment." [5] The same may be said of his wit,

---

3. Pope, *An Essay on Man,* III, lines 191–4, *An Essay on Criticism,* lines 741–4; John Pomfret, *The Choice* (1700), lines 108–11; Joseph Addison, *The Campaign, a Poem* (1705), lines 109–12.

4. *Poems,* I, 117–18.

5. *Correspondence,* I, 4–5 (Swift to Kendall, 11 February 1691/2). Cf. Bolingbroke's words to Ford (*Letters to Ford,* p. 240) some 30 years later: "The Dean's fancy is like that Devil which a certain Conjurer has rais'd, and which threaten'd to carry him away, if he left him for a moment unemploy'd." Swift seems to have been fond of repeating the remark to his friends.

which turned at times rather tediously to the bagatelle and the whim, to Latino-Anglicus or the Literalia style. Often the mischief could be turned to good purpose. We read in a letter to Stearne: "I am glad you made so good a progress in your building; but you had the emblem of industry in your mind, for the bees begin at the top and work downward, and at last work themselves out of house and home, as many of you builders do." In Gulliver's account of the Grand Academy of Lagado, this has become something pointed: "There was a most ingenious Architect who had contrived a new Method for building Houses, by beginning at the Roof, and working downwards to the Foundation; which he justified to me by the like Practice of those two prudent Insects, the Bee and the Spider." [6] Again we can see the tone of town gallantry which pervades the allegory of *A Tale of a Tub* in a letter written to Tisdall just before the *Tale* was published: "I wonder she [Stella] could be so wicked as to let the first word she could speak, after choking, be a pun. I differ from you; and believe the pun was just coming up, but met with the crumbs, and so, struggling for the wall, could neither of them get by, and at last came both out together." [7] What saved Swift from a career of literary mischief (such as the Scriblerus memoirs to a large extent remained) was a strong sense of design, a power to turn his wit to rhetorical ends. "You see I amuse myself *de la bagatelle* as much as you," wrote Boling-broke, "but here lies the difference, your *bagatelle* leads to something better, as fiddlers flourish carelessly, before they play a fine air, but mine begins, proceeds, and ends in *bagatelle*." [8]

THE EMERGENCE OF RHETORICAL METHOD

In Swift's early poems one can trace most easily the movement from a high style of wit to the rhetorical use of witty extravagance. The Pindaric odes have too often been dismissed as simply turgid flattery. They show a method of revaluation that includes sophistical argument but is based largely upon central oppositions of symbols. The "Ode to the Honorable Sir William Temple" may serve as an example. Its central figure is man unparadised; in the garden he was complete as he has never

6. *Correspondence*, I, 124 (30 November 1708); *Gulliver's Travels*, HD, XI, 164 (TS, VIII, 187).

7. *Correspondence*, I, 42 (3 February 1703/4). One may compare, too, Swift's remark in a letter of 1716 to Archbishop King (*ibid.*, II, 354)—"if we must suffer for a name, however, I had rather be devoured by a lion than a rat"—with his use of this figure in the second of the *Drapier's Letters*: "It is no Loss of Honour to submit to the *Lion*: But who, with the Figure of a *Man*, can think with Patience of being devoured alive by a *Rat?*" HD, X, 20 (TS, VI, 39).

8. *Correspondence*, III, 94 (21 July 1721).

been since. The fall of man is the loss of breadth of learning and common humanity, and the narrowness of pedantry and politicking is seen as the splintering of the original Adam. Man has fallen like Humpty Dumpty:

> *Virtue, the greatest of all Monarchies,*
> *Till its first Emperor rebellious Man*
> *Depos'd from off his Seat*
> *It fell, and broke with its own Weight*
> *Into small States and Principalities,*
> *By many a petty Lord possess'd,*
> *But ne'er since seated in one single Breast.*

Temple, to reconquer the empire of virtue, must rediscover it, for it survives only in the fragments of what man now calls learning. Some men have become pedants, scholar-fools, who spend their lives in a trivial alchemy, trying to turn their reading into "golden Rules." Others have become gamesters of state, who play at war and ply deep political designs. Temple alone has resisted the heresy that "knowledge forfeits all Humanity." He has achieved breadth of learning and has turned it to the uses of diplomacy rather than war. Now, tired of the inhuman court, he has retired to the garden where like Adam restored he can study nature's "innocent emblems" of society:

> *Where all the fruitful Atoms lye,*
> *How some go downward to the Root,*
> *Some more ambitiously upwards fly,*
> *And form the Leaves, the Branches, and the Fruit.*
> *You strove to cultivate a barren Court in vain,*
> *Your Garden's better worth your noble Pain,*
> *Hence Mankind fell, and here must rise again.*[9]

Swift is using a traditional theme: "The Earth is the Garden of Nature, and each fruitful Country a Paradise." Temple's withdrawal may remind us of Marvell's garden poems; in Swift, too, the garden represents in microcosm the ideal world of nature, with the atoms finding their proper place in the tree as man so often does not in the state.[1] The humanistic ideal of the whole man living in "country peace" is exalted by hyperbole to the image of paradise regained.

For all its pattern, the ode is rather heavy and disgressive. It has a calculated indirectness of manner, which Swift conceived as proper to the Pindaric form. In *The Battle of the Books* Pindar is shown "Never advancing in a direct Line, but wheeling with incredible Agility and

9. *Poems,* 1, 26, lines 1–7; 32, lines 171–7.
1. Thomas Browne, "Epistle Dedicatory," *The Garden of Cyrus* (London, 1658). Cf. Andrew Marvell, "Upon Appleton House, to My Lord Fairfax," xli, *Poems and Letters,* ed. H. M. Margoliouth (Oxford, Clarendon Press, 1927), 1, 69.

Force." [2] He is, moreover, the "fierce Ancient," and his manner is one of the few accommodations the new age allowed the enthusiastic spirit. The Pindaric manner is the meditative counterpart of the heroic style, and significantly enough, its enthusiasm turns largely to satirical fervor in Swift. But we must expect its tone to surpass the literal occasion; the apparent flattery of Temple is really the praise of the virtue which Temple has happened to recall and is used to symbolize. The method of the Pindarics because of its very principles never permitted the matrix of clear statement beneath which symbols might be suggested or the alternate method of ingenious argument from which they might be derived deductively.

In "Baucis and Philemon" the method of argument emerges with limited clarity. The poem seems in large measure a travesty of the pastoral hyperbole of Dryden's version of the myth. Dryden had deliberately played upon the irony of decent poverty as true wealth. His images came close to mock-heroic elaborations of Ovid's. A small kettle is magnified:

> *Like burnish'd gold the little seether shone.*

The white honeycomb set in the center of the table achieves regality in a court of attendant bowls:

> *All these a milk-white honey comb surround,*
> *Which in the midst the country banquet crown'd.*[3]

Swift, however, pays no attention to poverty. Instead of a single slice of bacon, "scarce enough for one," his cottagers have "large Slices" and "from the fattest Side." [4] Nor does the final metamorphosis of the pair into trees retain the mixture of wonder and pathos Dryden had given it. The amplification which Dryden gave to celebrating rural splendors Swift gives instead to insisting upon the commonplace realities of actual dull cottagers. This transformation is not unlike what Butler did with the metaphysical conceit. Dryden had used tender alexandrines:

> *Then, ere the bark above their shoulders grew,*
> *They give and take at once their last adieu;*
> *At once: "Farewell, O faithful spouse," they said;*
> *At once th'incroaching rinds their closing lips invade.*[5]

Instead of the death duet, Swift offers a dialogue that shows utter obliviousness to the nature of the experience:

2. HD, I, 158 (TS, I, 181).

3. John Dryden, "Baucis and Philemon," *Poetical Works,* p. 802, line 57; p. 803, lines 116–17. For further discussion of Swift's and Dryden's versions, see Maurice Johnson, *The Sin of Wit: Jonathan Swift as a Poet* (Syracuse, Syracuse University Press, 1950), pp. 89–92.

4. "The Story of Baucis and Philemon," *Poems,* I, 91, lines 59–60; 112, lines 27–8.

5. Dryden, *Poetical Works,* p. 804, lines 187–90.

> *When* Baucis *hastily cry'd out;*
> *My Dear, I see your Forehead sprout:*
> *Sprout, quoth the Man, What's this you tell us?*
> *I hope you don't believe me Jealous:*
> *But yet, methinks, I feel it true;*
> *And re'ly, Yours is budding too—*
> *Nay,—now I cannot stir my Foot:*
> *It feels as if 'twere taking Root.*[6]

For Dryden, the couple are nobler in spirit than their estate reveals, and the metamorphoses are, like the "canonization" of Pope's unfortunate lady, the wonderfully just fulfillment of their nature. In Swift, however, the couple change in estate only to remain the same dullards they were before. And the whole process of metamorphosis, house and all, emphasizes the theme:

> *The Chimny to a Steeple grown,*
> *The Jack would not be left alone*
> *But up against the Steeple rear'd,*
> *Became a Clock, and still adher'd,*
> *And still it's Love to Houshold Cares*
> *By a shrill Voice at Noon declares,*
> *Warning the Cook-maid not to burn*
> *That Roast-meat which it cannot turn.*
>
> *A Bed-sted in the antique mode*
> *Compos'd of Timber many a Load;*
> *Such as our Grandfathers did use,*
> *Was Metamorphos't into Pews;*
> *Which yet their former Virtue keep,*
> *By lodging Folks dispos'd to sleep.*[7]

The transformation of Baucis and Philemon is of the same sort; they gain new dress, new talk, new vanities, and no more. The second version of the poem, corrected by Addison, seems to suppress exuberance of detail only in order to give greater emphasis to this view of the parson as the same man in a new guise. The heart of the poem is the treatment of metamorphosis, which no longer confirms a spiritual quality by giving it proper embodiment but rather makes the new embodiment another vehicle for the same commonplace qualities. The whole process is therefore elaborately rationalized: that the jack *naturally* turns to a clock and the bed to pews are results of their similarity of function and serve to give that similarity stress. Instead of ennobling the humble and saying that low is really high, the method shows with debasing wit that high is after all the same as low.

In this reductive technique "Baucis and Philemon" approaches the

6. *Poems*, I, 116, lines 155–62.
7. *Ibid.*, I, 94, lines 139–52; 113, lines 74–84.

more abstract reasoning through metaphor that Swift had turned to satiric use in "The Description of a Salamander." This poem is in part an attack upon John Lord Cutts, known as the Salamander for his bravery under fire at the siege of Namur but regarded by Swift as the "vainest old fool alive." Even more, however, the poem uses Cutts as a typical instance of the extravagant reputation won by unworthy men and his sobriquet as an example of the cant of popular adulation:

> *For, what is understood by* Fame
> *Beside the getting of a Name?*

Swift goes about, therefore, fastening the name of Salamander on Cutts for new reasons; he cites Pliny's description and applies it:

> FIRST *then, our Author has defin'd*
> *This Reptil, of the Serpent kind,*
> *With gawdy Coat, and shining Train,*
> *But loathsom Spots his Body stain:*
> *Out from some Hole obscure he flies*
> *When Rains descend, and Tempests rise,*
> *Till the Sun clears the Air; and then*
> *Crawls back neglected to his Den.*

> *So when the War has rais'd a Storm*
> *I've seen a* Snake *in human Form,*
> *All stain'd with Infamy and Vice,*
> *Leap from the Dunghill in a trice,*
> *Burnish and make a gaudy show,*
> *Become a General, Peer and Beau,*
> *Till Peace hath made the Sky serene,*
> *Then shrink into it's Hole again.*

> All this we grant—why, then look yonder
> Sure that must be a *Salamander!* [8]

The images which are generated in the analogy—war as a storm which upsets normal values, peace as the serene sky and, implicitly, the return of reason—help to enforce Swift's attitude and give it point. But the primary device is Swift's arguing from irrelevant attributes of a metaphor to reverse the customary judgment. The epithet of Salamander is a term capable, in Swift's hands, of startling ambiguity, yet its novel meanings are carefully reasoned.

We can see this method in a better poem, the satire on Marlborough, "The Fable of Midas" (like "Baucis and Philemon" a travesty of an Ovidian story):

> Midas, *we are in Story told,*
> *Turn'd ev'ry thing he touch't to* Gold:

8. *Ibid.*, 1, 83, lines 13–14; 83–4, lines 29–46. Cf. "Apollo's Edict," *ibid.*, 1, 270, lines 18–19: "And when you'd make a Heroe grander, Forget he's like a *Salamander.*"

> *He* chip't *his* Bread, *the Pieces round*
> *Glitter'd like Spangles on the Ground:*
> *A Codling e'er it went his Lip in,*
> *Would strait become a* Golden *Pippin*
>
> .   .   .   .
>
> *Whene'er he chanc'd his Hands to lay,*
> *On Magazines of* Corn *or* Hay,
> Gold *ready Coin'd appear'd, instead*
> *Of Paultry* Provender *and* Bread :
> *Hence we are by wise Farmers told,*
> Old *Hay* is equal to old *Gold;*
> *And hence a Critick deep maintains,*
> *We learn't to weigh our* Gold *by* Grains.

The last four lines are typical of the false wit we have seen in the Salamander poem; the testimony of a farmer's saw or of a critic's philology is
speciously introduced, by the lightest sophistry, to make the fable coherent
with accepted truths. The description of Midas, with ass's ears, in the
river is an even better case of a passage shaped to prepare for the application derived from it.

> *Against whose Torrent while he Swims,*
> *The* Golden *Scurf peels off his Limbs:*
> *Fame spreads the News, and People travel*
> *From far, to gather* golden *Gravel;*
> Midas, *expos'd to all their Jears,*
> *Had lost his* Art, *and kept his* Ears.

Having plotted his parallels, Swift can move effortlessly to the account
of Marlborough's being deprived of command. The Senate, seeking to
scour the "British Midas' dirty Paws," washes away his *"Chymick*
Power."

> *While He his utmost Strength apply'd,*
> *To Swim against this* Pop'lar *Tide,*
> *The* Golden *Spoils flew off apace,*
> *Here fell a* Pension, *there a* Place
>
> .   .   .   .   .   .
>
> *And* Midas *now neglected stands*
> *With* Asses Ears, *and dirty Hands.*[9]

These poems show the peculiar force of Swift's use of wit. He gives
contempt the formality of argument, but the formal argument only pretends to prove while it accommodates the charge in another way. By
transforming a stock identification or creating a new one which fits at
many points, Swift can assume the manner of deducing his conclusions.
The identification, not the poet, requires them. These small allegorical

9. *Ibid.,* I, 156, lines 1–6, 15–22; 157, lines 35–40; 158, lines 73–6, 81–2.

structures, with their elaborate rationalization, have something in common with the mock-heroic. Just as the satirist may refuse to grant his victims less than heroic intentions (for each age must have its heroes, and these are the men of loudest profession) and can fix them thereby in a pattern which overwhelms them, so here Swift fashions a pattern that is irresistibly imposed by verbal and pictorial aptness and carefully designed to debase those it seems to fit. If the pattern is to be rejected, we must decide at which point the fable is misapplied. Yet the fable seems to insist upon its applicability at some level, and all of the implicit judgments which its terms suggest must be brought to consciousness as we decide. We may reject the simplification of the fable or not, but at least we must encounter and test it fully.

FALSE WIT IN THE PROSE

The method of false wit persists in Swift's prose throughout his career, although it becomes an occasional rather than a central technique after *A Tale of a Tub*. It is used as a critical technique of meeting false rhetoric with even falser rhetoric, of turning the pretensions of an opponent into self-accusations. Nowhere else does Swift accomplish this task with more economy and ebullience than in his reply to Bishop Burnet. The passage has much in common with that on the dissenters and with the poem on Cutts, but its peculiar distinction is Swift's elaborate conversion of Burnet's own terms.

Swift derides Burnet's fears of the Pretender and Popery and denounces Burnet's use of those fears to urge toleration to dissenters as fellow Protestants. Finally he takes some of Burnet's most intense figures and turns them upon the author:

However, he "thanks God there are many among us who stand in the breach:" I believe they may; 'tis a breach of their own making, and they design to come forward, and storm and plunder, if they be not driven back. "They make themselves a wall for their church and country." A south wall, I suppose, for all the best fruit of the church and country to be nailed on. Let us examine this metaphor: The wall of our church and country is built of those who love the constitution in both: Our domestic enemies undermine some parts of the wall, and place themselves in the breach; and then they cry, "We are the wall!" We do not like such patchwork, they build with untempered mortar; nor can they ever cement with us, till they get better materials and better workmen: God keep us from having our breaches made up with such rubbish! "They stand upon the watchtower;" they are indeed pragmatical enough to do so; but who assigned them that post, to give us false intelligence, to alarm us with false dangers, and send us to defend one gate, while their accomplices are breaking in at another? "They cry to God, day and night to avert the judgment of Popery which seems to hasten towards us." Then I affirm, they are hypocrites by day, and filthy dreamers by night. When they cry unto him, he will not hear them: For they cry against the plainest dictates of their own conscience, reason, and belief.

But lastly, "They lie in the dust, mourning before him." Hang me if I believe that, unless it be figuratively spoken. But suppose it to be true; why do "they lie in the dust?" Because they love to raise it: For what do "they mourn?" Why, for power, wealth, and places. There let the enemies of the Queen, and monarchy, and the church, lie, and mourn, and lick the dust, like serpents, till they are truly sensible of their ingratitude, falsehood, disobedience, slander, blasphemy, sedition, and every evil work! [1]

The wit of the passage depends largely on its economy of means. Serious as Swift's accusation is, his cheerful emphasis on the verbalism of the whole performance—"Hang me if I believe that, unless it be figuratively spoken"—only points to the cheapness of Burnet's appeal; and the harsh invective with which the passage ends is as hyperbolic as Burnet's professed fears. Wit is here used destructively; its crazy reconstruction is more a parody of Burnet's rhetoric than an answer.

Counteraccusation such as this approaches paradox, and we can see it going all the way at the close of one of the *Examiner* papers. There Swift makes a startling attack upon the Whigs as the real allies of "Popery, Arbitrary Power, and the Pretender." The effect is not unlike that of charging the Commons with "tyranny," but this paper culminates in a dazzling passage:

A Dog loves to turn round often; yet after certain *Revolutions,* he lies down to *Rest:* But Heads, under the Dominion of the *Moon,* are for perpetual *Changes,* and perpetual *Revolutions:* Besides, the *Whigs* owe all their Wealth to *Wars* and *Revolutions;* like the girl at *Bartholomew-Fair,* who gets a Penny by turning round a hundred Times, with Swords in her Hands.[2]

This makes no claim of logical strictness; it is held together by deliberate shifts of meaning and false analogies. But both the shifts and the analogies have their own method. Wars and revolutions are implicitly identified with the perpetual restlessness of the lunatic, and the restlessness of lunacy is in turn unfavorably compared with the motion of a beast

1. *A Preface to the B——p of S——r——m's Introduction to the Third Volume of the History of the Reformation of the Church of England, by Gregory Misosarum,* TS, iii, 159–60. For the passage on the dissenters, see above, chap. ii, pp. 22–4.

2. *Examiner,* No. 39 (3 May 1711), HD, iii, 147 (TS, ix, 261).

(which at least behaves according to the laws of nature and occasionally rests). Once the action of the Whigs is branded as unnatural, its motives are examined; for all that is unnatural is presumably caused by interest or passion. Here Swift finds a figure which at once symbolizes both wars and revolution, the girl turning with swords in her hands. The usefulness of the symbol lies, however, not merely in its pictorial aptness, for the subsidiary implications are of greater weight. The girl's action is profitless except to herself; it is merely a curious feat of charlatanry performed for the sake of money.

The last paragraph in this *Examiner* paper uses less concrete imagery, but it plays on the term "pretender" as the preceding one did on "revolution."

> To conclude, the *Whigs,* have a natural Faculty of bringing in *Pretenders,* and will therefore probably endeavour to bring in the great One at last: How many *Pretenders* to Wit, Honour, Nobility, Politicks, have they brought in these last twenty Years? In short, they have been sometimes able to procure a Majority of *Pretenders* in Parliament; and wanted nothing to render the Work compleat, except a *Pretender* at their Head.[3]

Freed from its limitation in meaning to the claimant to the throne, the word "pretender" becomes mercurial and calls up all the associations which Swift has prepared for it earlier. Thus it suggests the false party wits, the new rich who have profited by the war, new heroes and noblemen like Marlborough. Swift's image of the Whigs is one of men with no loyalties but to themselves, men who have gained through wealth the power that belonged to birth, property, or natural virtue. The connection of these pretenders with the actual Pretender depends upon a pun, and the charge is preposterous, although not too much more so than the same charge made against the Tories. But beneath the lightness of false wit, and really by means of it, Swift has evoked a serious view of the Whigs which undercuts all their charges. It is a view, reinforced by suggestions of charlatanry and usurpation, of a moneyed class without traditional loyalties aspiring to the dignities of an aristocracy and threatening thereby the stability of the nation and of its culture.

The force of Swift's wit depends upon range as well as economy; indeed, the economy becomes valuable only in proportion to the weight of values supported in its pivotal terms. One source of such weight is allusion, to traditional literary prototypes of the present situation or even more, since their import is more familiar and more resonant, to the Biblical counterparts. In his reply to Burnet, Swift reduces the bishop's scriptural allusions to nonsense, but Swift often makes good use of

3. *Ibid.*

them himself to extend the terms of his contrast and to reveal the full
measure of incongruity between profession and motive, duty and act. In
The Drapier's Letters, particularly, where the audience is popular and
the problem a conflict of morality and expediency, Swift makes frequent
and powerful allusions to the Bible. At the opening of the fourth of the
letters, addressed to the "whole people of Ireland," he tries to awaken
moral sense by making its loss a matter of precise and inescapable judgment:

> A People long used to Hardships, lose by Degrees the very Notions
> of *Liberty;* they look upon themselves as Creatures at Mercy; and that
> all Impositions laid on them by a stronger Hand, are, in the Phrase
> of the *Report, legal* and *obligatory.* Hence proceed that *Poverty* and
> *Lowness of Spirit,* to which a *Kingdom* may be subject, as well as a
> *particular Person.* And when *Esau* came fainting from the Field, at
> the Point to die, it is no Wonder that he sold his *Birth-Right for a Mess
> of Pottage.*[4]

The dry phrase, "it is no Wonder" (comparable to the more frequent
"they had Reason"), is the pivot between a relaxing sympathy and the
moral severity of such words as St. Paul's:

> Look diligently lest any man fail of the grace of God; lest any root of
> bitterness springing up trouble you, and thereby many be defiled;
> Lest there be any fornicator, or profane person, as Esau, who for
> one morsel of meat sold his birthright.
> For ye know that afterward, when he would have inherited the
> blessing, he was rejected: for he found no place of repentance, though
> he sought it carefully with tears.[5]

In the Drapier's attack upon William Wood we can see how essential
to his rhetoric Swift's wit can be. All its uses are brought to bear—its
reductive power, its method of implication, its weight of allusion. The
initial task of the Drapier was to discredit Wood, whose copper halfpence (his "brass") were to be forced upon the Irish in quantities potentially so great as to drain off their gold and silver. It was not Wood
himself that mattered; his figure became the symbol of the unjust pretensions of the English ministry. Walpole and Townshend, unable to
believe that Wood's patent would do Ireland real economic harm, saw
in Irish resistance only an attack upon royal prerogative and upon the
political dependency of Ireland.[6] The Drapier, in elevating Wood to

4. HD, x, 53 (TS, vi, 101).
5. *Hebrews* 12:15-17.
6. A. Goodwin, "Wood's Halfpence," *English Historical Review, 51* (1936), 647-75
esp. pp. 668-9. This article presents the best discussion of the issues at stake and in
cludes valuable extracts from contemporary correspondence. See also *The Drapier'*
Letters to the People of Ireland, ed. Herbert Davis (Oxford, Clarendon Press, 1935)

an "arbitrary Mock-Monarch," dissociated the will of the actual king, who was presumed to be just, from the unjust force used in Wood's name. It was left to George and to his ministers to disavow Wood or to acknowledge the injustice as their own. In two poems written at the time Swift cultivated this theme of the usurpation of just authority by a fool. In one Wood became a mock Prometheus, who stole the golden chain of Jove (in order to coin it for himself) and substituted a slack "brazen String." In another Wood became a Phaeton-like figure, Salmoneus, the "mad Copper-smith of Elis," who drove brass-shod steeds before a brazen car in the hope that the Irish would mistake the "noise of brass" for Jove's true thunder.[7] In the *Letters* themselves the Drapier uses wit to create a nice balance between contempt and indignation: Wood is absurd, but he can become terrible if he is not resisted.

Wood, the Drapier insists, is a "poor, private, obscure Mechanick." His impudence and imposition are ridiculous, but their success is even more so:

> for sure there was never an Example in History, of a great Kingdom kept in Awe for above a Year, in daily Dread of utter Destruction; not by a powerful Invader at the Head of Twenty thousand Men; not by a Plague or a Famine; not by a tyrannical Prince (for we never had one more Gracious) or a corrupt Administration; but by one single, diminutive, insignificant Mechanick.[8]

Again and again the dissociation of Wood from the true monarch is insistently made:

> Mr. *Wood* will *Oblige* me to take Five-pence Half-penny of his Brass in every payment. And I will shoot Mr. *Wood* and his Deputies through the Head, like *High-way Men* or *House-breakers,* if they dare to force one Farthing of their Coin on me in the Payment of an Hundred Pounds. It is no Loss of Honour to submit to the *Lion:* But who, with the Figure of a *Man,* can think with Patience of being devoured alive by a *Rat?*

In separating tyrannical mechanic from gracious prince and rat from royal lion, the Drapier could assure his countrymen that they had "all the Laws of God and Man" on their side: "it is but saying *No,* and you are safe." A highwayman with no power was but a madman.[9]

Once the legality of Wood's patent was asserted by the king's Privy Council, the target of the attack was shifted to the powers that so obviously lay behind Wood's own insignificant figure. The dissociation now

7. "Prometheus, a Poem," *Poems,* I, 343–7; "On Wood the Iron-Monger," *Poems,* I, 352–3.
8. HD, x, 19 (TS, VI, 38).
9. HD, x, 20, 23 (TS, VI, 39, 42).

to be made was between legality and justice, and nowhere did the Drapier's allusions become more bitter:

> St. *Paul* says, *All Things are* lawful, *but all Things are not* expedient We are answered that this Patent is *lawful;* but is it *expedient?* We read, that the high Priest said, *It was expedient that one Man should die for the People;* and this was a most wicked Proposition. But that a *whole Nation* should *die for one Man,* was never heard of before.[1]

Not even the judgment of Caiaphas, the Drapier seems to be saying—and you honor Wood as you should your Lord—not even that was as callous as yours. This inversion of righteousness sets the tone for the fine passage at the close of the third letter:

> I am very sensible, that such a Work as I have undertaken, might have worthily employed a much better Pen. But when a House is attempted to be robbed, it often happens that the weakest in the Family, runs first to stop the Door. . . . I was in the Case of *David,* who *could not move in the Armour of* Saul; and therefore I rather chose to attack this *uncircumcised Philistine* (*Wood* I mean) *with a Sling and a Stone.* And I may say for *Wood*'s Honour, as well as my own, that he resemble *Goliah* in many Circumstances, very applicable to the present Purpose For *Goliah* had *a Helmet of* Brass *upon his Head, and he was armed with a Coat of Mail, and the Weight of the Coat was five Thousand Shekles of* Brass, *and he had Greaves of* Brass *upon his Legs, and a Target of* Brass *between his Shoulders.* In short, he was like Mr *Wood,* all over Brass; and *he defied the Armies of the living God Goliah's* Conditions of Combat were likewise the same with those of *Wood: If he prevail against us, then we shall be his Servants.* But if it happen that I *prevail* over him, I renounce the other Part of the Conditions; he shall never be a *Servant* of mine; for I do not think him fit to be trusted in any *honest* Man's Shop.[2]

Wood is here represented as the invader, the enemy of the "Armies of the living God," impressive enough in mere power to discourage the Irish "When Saul and all Israel heard those words of the Philistine, they were dismayed, and greatly afraid." The Drapier in turn becomes the champion of righteousness, successful against odds, "for the battle is the Lord's." Swift's lightness of logical connections gives the passage its surprises he turns from the Drapier's lack of learning to David's inability to support Saul's armor, from the combat of David with Goliath to the likenesses of Wood and Goliath. Finally he shifts from the metaphorical level back to the literal situation. If Goliath is to be construed as Wood

1. HD, x, 41 (TS, vi, 80).
2. HD, x, 48 (TS, vi, 90-1).

the metaphor can be taken only so far: Wood is a mock Goliath, too contemptible and dishonest to be a worthy captive in defeat. This device, the reductive shift from metaphor to the literal situation, from the field of combat to the Drapier's shop, resembles the treatment of Bishop Burnet's figures. It has the rhetorical effect of pointing to the falseness of the whole issue: Wood, unlike Goliath, has no power of his own and is at best a preposterous instrument of the English ministry. Wood's case so completely lacks justification that it cannot be taken seriously in its own terms; yet it is only in its own terms that Walpole can push it or that Swift is willing to consider it. The allusion, moreover, has heightened the controversy to a battle of right against power, leaving power only a mock Goliath as its pretense to a just champion.

The method of wit, then, persists as a powerful rhetorical technique; the bagatelle leads to something better. To an extent the method of wit resembles that of the plain style; both present an appearance of logical progression and conceal their deviation from an expected line of reasoning. Somewhere there is a point of bifurcation, and in the surprise at the conclusion we may wish to find it in order to go where we had expected to be. Or we may find that we have arrived where we should be and wish to see where our original error had been. In either case, we are awakened to more than we could have expected or even wished. Yet for all these similarities the two methods have notable differences. The method of wit achieves a more striking economy. Its reversal is accomplished within a single word, by whatever means. There is less of the deliberate preparation of terms we have seen in the plain style, more deliberate effrontery to the claims of logical strictness. The reversal often is a more radical one. Wit may use more calculated incongruity. These devices are the means whereby wit calls attention to itself, and this ostentation of sophistry, which had provided both a defiance and a complement to rational argument for the metaphysicals, sets off false wit from true for the Augustans.

The sophistry of Augustan false wit has lost any overtones of piety, and it has become all the more self-assertive as a result. The typical instance in Swift has a surface of excessive rationalization which only points to the verbal play that sustains it; and the verbal play must in turn be rationalized anew, at a deeper level of awareness. The peculiar quality of this wit is its tireless ingenuity in fusing rigidity of form (syllogistic statement or the heavily rhymed Hudibrastic meter) with a protean disordering of words. The meanings of words shift to fit the syllogism; their sounds are controlled by the demands of meter. The low style becomes the Augustans' parody of the order of true wit: it is an order hardened into mechanism, dislocating meanings for the sake of form. Yet the triumph of this wit is the plasticity it gives to word and image. The dislocations they seem helplessly to endure are the calculated means of re-

ordering our experience with sudden insight, of turning our attention
from the brightness of the brass to the serpent within:

> For the poor ignorant people, allured by the appearing convenience in
> their small dealings, did not discover the serpent in the brass, but were
> ready, like the Israelites, to offer incense to it; neither could the wis-
> dom of the nation convince them, until some, of good intentions, made
> the cheat so plain to their sight, that those who run may read.[3]

3. *Doing Good*, HD, ix, 238 (TS, iv, 187).

IV

The Ironic Mask

FROM ANALYSIS TO IRONY

IN THE reversals of wit two opposed meanings converge in a potentially ambiguous term. We approach the term with one meaning and leave it with another. The irony we associate with Swift has much in common with this. As John F. Ross has explained, the "irony exists not alone in the 'literal' meaning, nor alone in the 'hidden' or 'intended' meaning; it is the effect of the two meanings emerging in simultaneous relationship. That is, *A* (the 'literal' meaning) + *B* (the 'intended' meaning) make up *C* (the ironic effect). In this regard, irony has the same basic structure as metaphor." [1] We have two different kinds of condensation, both verbal but one horizontal and the other vertical. In the case of wit two terms merge in a common property; we move readily from one to the other as we might move in a dream or a film from one room to another through the picture that each has on its wall. In irony we hear two voices, one saying what its limited character requires, the other what a different awareness must add or oppose. The quality of the ironic effect will be determined by the relationship of these two voices —the extent to which they differ, the degree to which one complements the other or simply discredits it, the range of attitudes which can be inferred as the ground for each.

The same apparent incongruity and ultimate reconciliation we find in metaphor occur here, but in irony they occur as a meeting of levels. From another approach irony might be regarded as condensed antithesis, expressed not in the balance of two terms but in the balance of two meanings simultaneously expressed in one term. The expanded form of antithesis is the typical note of such a style as Addison's: "We are apt to rely upon future Prospects, and become really expensive while we are only rich in Possibility." [2] Swift's method is generally less direct. In his ironic works he creates a series of speakers, each of them unaware of one term of a possible antithesis and all the more unguarded, because of this obtuseness, in calling attention to what he disregards. The author of *A Tale of a Tub* complains bathetically to Prince Posterity of the malice of

1. John F. Ross, *Swift and Defoe: A Study in Literary Relationship* (Berkeley, University of California Press, 1941), pp. 81–2.
2. *Spectator*, No. 191 (9 October 1711).

Time: "The *never-dying* Works of these illustrious Persons, Your *Governour*, Sir, has devoted to unavoidable Death." From there he goes on to an unwitting damnation of his contemporaries: "His inveterate Malice is such to the Writings of our Age, that of several Thousands produced yearly from this renowned City, before the next Revolution of the Sun, there is not one to be heard of: Unhappy Infants, many of them barbarously destroyed before they have so much as learnt their *Mother-Tongue* to beg for Pity." In striving for pathos the Tale Teller has neglected the commonplace we can find in Hobbes: "Children therefore are not endued with Reason at all, till they have attained the use of Speech." [3]

The ironist must give this obtuseness significance; the structure of the whole work gives point to the particular blindness of a single remark. "There are solecisms in morals," Swift wrote bitterly to Steele, "as well as in language." [4] And the creation of an obtuse speaker allows the two to merge; the insensitivity to meanings serves to characterize a moral blindness. Swift's description of Tindall's *Rights of the Christian Church* might apply very well to *A Tale of a Tub* if one were to stop at its surface meaning: "It is a Treatise wholly devoid of Wit or Learning, under the most violent and weak Endeavours and Pretences to both." For the *Tale* Swift deliberately creates a master of both kinds of solecism, of "impudent Sophistry," "false Logick," and "factious Jargon." The function of the speaker also is well stated in Swift's remarks on Tindall: "It is hard to think sometimes whether this Man is hired to write for or against Dissenters and the sects. This is their Opinion, although they will not own it so roundly." The obtuse speaker does not know enough to put a respectable face on his cause; he gives away his own folly and the interest he serves, where the wiser knave might successfully deceive. [5]

The obtuseness in itself is the first concern of Swift, for it is the absence of objective good sense in the style that arouses doubt about the author's character. Tindall and Richard Steele, as Swift portrays them, are the very reverse of what a writer should be. Tindall has a "Talent of rattling out Phrases, which seem to have sense, but have none at all." The same is true of Steele: "He has a confused remembrance of words since he left the university, but has lost half their meaning, and puts them together with no regard but to their cadence; as I remember a fellow nailed up maps in a gentleman's closet, some sideling, others upside down, the

---

3. HD, I, 20 (TS, I, 35). Hobbes, *Leviathan*, Pt. I, chap. v.

4. *Correspondence*, II, 35 (23 May 1713).

5. *Remarks upon a Book Intitled "The Rights of the Christian Church, &c.,"* HD, II, 72, 102 (TS, III, 87, 119). Cf. the remarks on the Earl of Wharton: "He is without the Sense of Shame or Glory, as some Men are without the Sense of Smelling; and therefore, a good Name to him is no more than a precious Ointment would be to these. *A Short Character of Thomas Earl of Wharton*, HD, III, 178 (TS, v, 8).

better to adjust them to the panels." [6] This corruption of language, for Swift as for Pope, is a token of the decline of a culture, and the growth of cant words is "the most ruinous corruption in any language." For cant reflects the growth of sect and faction, of the peculiar slavery of modishness and the necessary surrender of critical reflection or indeed of thought itself. Swift's London always had "one or more dunces of figure, who had credit enough to give use to some new word, and propagate in most conversations, though it had neither humor nor significancy." Stupidity was bad enough in itself, but it provided entrance for much more. However lightly Swift might remark to Pope of a contemporary that he was "a damnable poet, and consequently a public enemy to mankind," there was something of the Platonic sense that the poet can pervert the state. The acceptance of the cant of poets prepared for the acceptance of all cant, in politics or religion as well.[7]

In Swift's attacks upon Steele we can see the destructive analysis which prepares for the ironic construction. In his exposure of solecisms we can see more clearly his ironic purpose in inventing them. Swift claims to "strip some of [Steele's] insinuations from their generality and solecisms, and drag them into the light." Where Steele "endeavours to mould up his rancour and civility together," Swift scrapes off "his good manners, in order to come at his meaning which lies under." First Steele's "complicated ignorance" must be penetrated, then his "peculiar strain" reduced to sense. The inept figure may be turned back upon itself, as were those of Burnet:

> He asks himself whether "Popery and Ambition are become tame and quiet neighbours?" In this I can give him no satisfaction, because I never was in that street where they live; nor do I converse with any of their friends; only I find they are persons of a very evil reputation. But I am told for certain that Ambition has removed her lodging, and lives the very next door to Faction; where they keep such a racket that the whole parish is disturbed, and every night in an uproar.[8]

Each of Steele's insinuations is run down: it must be "by a figure of speech" that Steele calls his assertions in the *Guardian* (a mere "penny paper to be read in coffeehouses") "laying things before the ministry." [9] In the same way the professions of Steele's master Burnet are exposed as the romantic delusion of a depraved imagination:

6. On Tindall, HD, II, 78 (TS, III, 93); on Steele, *The Public Spirit of the Whigs,* TS, V, 321.
7. TS, X, 19; TS, XI, 11; *Correspondence,* IV, 60 (6 March 1728/9). The poet to whom Swift refers is Richard Daniel.
8. TS, V, 325, 331, 343.
9. *The Importance of the Guardian Considered,* TS, V, 294.

I am an old man, "a preacher above fifty years," and I now expect and am ready to die a martyr for the doctrines I have preached. What an amiable idea does he here leave upon our minds, of Her Majesty and her government! He has been poring so long upon Fox's Book of Martyrs, that he imagines himself living in the reign of Queen Mary, and is resolved to set up for a knight-errant against Popery.[1]

The ease with which Swift converts an ennobling term into a degrading one points to the ineptitude with which it has been used. As Swift puts it, he must "melt this refined Jargon into the *Old Style,* for the Improvement of such, who are not enough conversant in the *New.*" [2]

Nowhere is this melting accomplished to better purpose than in the reply to Anthony Collins, whose *Discourse of Free-Thinking* Swift put into "Plain English . . . for the Use of the Poor." Collins was no fool; he was well aware of what he was doing. In attacking the dogma by which the church held power over men he advocated "free thinking," but his use of the term was artfully duplicitous. In its more general sense it meant the use of reason unrestrained by authority to test all evidence, and it could be attributed to any questioner of false tradition, even Christ and St. Paul. But, as Richard Bentley remarked, Collins "thinks *Freedom of Thought* to be then only exercis'd, when it dissents and opposes." [3] Once he had gained a benign import for free thinking, Collins simply limited its use to skeptical rejection of all dogma. Swift's method of reply was to summarize concisely Collins' *Discourse,* amplifying at intervals in order to make the abuse of the key term clear. One example will serve, Swift's summary of Collins on Socrates, with Swift's interpolations italicized:

Socrates was a freethinker; for he disbelieved the gods of his country, and the common creeds about them, and declared his dislike when he heard men attribute "repentance, anger, and other passions to the gods, and talk of wars and battles in heaven, and of the gods getting women with child," and such like fabulous and blasphemous stories. *I pick out these particulars, because they are the very same with what the priests have in their Bibles, where repentance and anger are attributed to God; where it is said, there was "war in heaven;" and that "the Virgin Mary was with child by the Holy Ghost," whom the priests call God; all fabulous and blasphemous stories.* Now, I affirm Socrates to have been a true Christian. You will ask, perhaps, how that can be, since he lived three or four hundred years before Christ? I answer, with Justin Martyr, that Christ is nothing else but reason, and I hope you do not think Socrates lived before reason. Now, this true Chris-

1. TS, III, 158.
2. The words are written of Tindall, HD, II, 80 (TS, III, 96).
3. Richard Bentley, *Remarks upon a Late Discourse of Free-Thinking* (London, 1713), p. 12.

tian Socrates never made notions, speculations, or mysteries, any part of his religion, but demonstrated all men to be fools who troubled themselves with enquiries into heavenly things. Lastly, 'tis plain that Socrates was a freethinker, because he was calumniated for an atheist, as freethinkers generally are, *only because he was an enemy to all speculations and inquiries into heavenly things. For I argue thus, that if I never trouble myself to think whether there be a God or no, and forbid others to do it, I am a freethinker, but not an atheist.*[4]

In Swift's "Introduction" to the abstract, written in the manner of a dedicated Whig, we can see the creation of an ironic mask to accompany the views he has ridiculed. He provides a context for Collins' views by showing not only their atheistic consequences but also their political counterpart. There is considerable unfairness, as editors have observed, in the attribution of Collins' views to the Whig party, but it is certainly doubtful that Swift's attribution was offered for simple credulity. He himself warns, as the Church of England Man, against simple identifications of this sort, for "every Extreme . . . flings a general Scandal upon the whole Body it pretends to adhere to." Such scandal is undeserved unless the "practices" of the body "do openly, and without the least Room for Doubt, contradict [its] Profession."[5] Here Swift is not a mere propagandist; the introduction is clearly ironic. He is, however, challenging the Whigs to change their practices or to risk the scandal.

Finally, the introduction applies the subtitle, "Put into Plain English . . . for the Use of the Poor," with typical incisiveness: "I could see no reason why these great discoveries should be hid from our youth of quality, who frequent White's and Tom's; why they should not be adapted to the capacities of the Kit-Cat and Hanover Clubs, who might then be able to read lectures on them to their several toasts." While he parodies the false charity of the self-seeking reformer, he suggests that "the poor" are properly the semiliterate, fashionable youth who find their distinction in advanced views. Nor is it only the coffeehouse followers who are the true poor. The abstracter has added "some few explanations of [his] own, where the terms happen to be too learned, and consequently a little beyond the comprehension of those for whom the

4. *Mr. C——ns's Discourse of Free-Thinking*, TS, III, 185–6. According to Collins, Socrates not only declared his disbelief in the ancient gods "but obtain'd a just Notion of the Nature and Attributes of God, exactly agreeable to that which we have receiv'd by Divine Revelation, and became a true *Christian* (if it be allow'd that the Primitive Fathers understood what true Christianity was). . . . [Socrates asked] Inquirers whether they had attain'd a perfect knowledge of Human things since they search'd into Heavenly things; or if they could think themselves wise in neglecting that which concern'd them, to employ themselves in that which was above their capacity to understand." Anthony Collins, *A Discourse of Free-Thinking* (London, 1713), pp. 123–4, 125–6.

5. HD, II, 4 (TS, III, 53–4).

work was principally intended, I mean the nobility and gentry of our party." [6] This is Swift's familiar twist of the knife: Collins' discourse is in effect a Whig pamphlet, but it must be turned into more familiar terms so that the Whigs can understand it and recognize its value to them. They must be made to see what they have espoused and to face the full truth without a disguise of comfortable obscurity.

Swift's criticism, then, turns readily from analysis to ironic parody. The ironic method allows a constant implication of motive: solecisms of language and solecisms of morals steadily reinforce each other. The character of the speaker discredits his words, and his words in turn characterize him. One value of the method is that its continuity is not broken by the striking local effects of false wit; the reversals which these might achieve individually are made an essential part of the whole design. The use of levels of meaning in irony—the vertical method of wit—keeps us aware of incongruity yet allows the individual solecisms to be woven into a fabric of consistent attitudes and character. The effects of wit are muted by their second function; they have now become flashes of characterization as well. The complete reversal, suggested throughout, is suspended, as in *Gulliver's Travels,* to the end. As a result the ironically sustained solecisms grow into a complex embodiment of a deficient moral attitude, and about the central attitude may be clustered others that give it density. In the case of Collins, we can see the cant of deism associated both with a Whiggish disregard of the religious foundation of the state and with the dullness of the monied gentry who are furthering ends they hardly recognize. The fusion is not complete in the tract on Collins, but in *A Modest Proposal* or *Gulliver's Travels* Swift achieves a unity which makes each element serve a multiplicity of purposes.

The Creation of the Mask

"The generality of the world writ[e] in a mask and the want of a true knowledge of the humour of people on your side the water, cause many errors on this." So Archbishop King wrote to Swift from Dublin in 1708. Six years later, Arbuthnot wrote from London of a new pamphlet: "This by a flaming Jacobite, that wonders all the world are not so. Perhaps it may be a Whig, that personates a Jacobite." [7] In Arbuthnot's remark one can see an extreme toward which irony works, what we call today "black propaganda." To forge statements by an enemy which might discredit him is a common enough practice, only more elaborate than to misquote an opponent or to distort his meaning. But such forgery intro-

---

6. TS, III, 170–1.
7. *Correspondence,* I, 107; II, 175. Cf. *Examiner,* No. 19 (14 December 1710), HD, III, 36 (TS, IX, 116), from "I here declare" to end of paragraph.

duces the new element of impersonation, of assuming convincingly a character other than one's own. The ironist must also make clear that he is ironic. He must be recognizable but inacceptable; we must know who he pretends to be, but we must know that he is only pretending. We must not only recognize the mask, we must also recognize that it is a mask.

It is for this reason that the ironist is generally limited to assuming a typical personality, a character clearly defined by social or literary convention. The tradition of the Theophrastan character had for Swift's age defined moral types; the drama had created its humor characters and given them the further trappings of a social position. The fop was a social type as well as a humor; the vain man was often a soldier or pedant. Social types, moreover, acquire distinctive patterns of speech, such as Ben Jonson distinguished and exploited. Swift could write two pages of wordplay in which "a number of People of different Conditions" express their rage against William Wood.

> *Nurse.* I'll *Swaddle* him.
> *Anabaptist.* We'll *dip* the Rogue in the *Pond.*
> *Ostler.* I'll *rub* him down. . . .
> *Gamester.* I'll make his *Bones rattle.*
> *Bodice-maker.* I'll *lace* his Sides.
> *Gardener.* I'll make him *water his Plants.*
> *Ale-wife.* I'll *reckon* with him.[8]

It is this interest in the idioms of his day that has made his *Polite Conversation* a treasure for the lexicographer. Swift, for the most part, condemned idiosyncratic cant, but he often regarded it with a mixed horror and affection, much as the collector might. Like Swift, for example, W. H. Auden can assume with precision the tone of a typical contemporary, whether a prize-day speaker, a vicar confusing his passions with his conscience, or a tortured liberal in the person of Herod.[9] But more than the modern poet, Swift could work in a tradition of formalized "character" writing and of a drama which preserved much of the Jonsonian humor; he was writing in an age which through the periodical essay created the morally and socially defined character that grew to be Fielding's Parson Adams or Squire Western. Swift's was an age of norms, even norms of abnormality.

The typical was established, as early as Aristotle's *Rhetoric,* by criteria which were largely moral. The subtle psychology of the seventeenth century, such as we find in La Rochefoucauld or Halifax and in men as different as Henry More or Thomas Hobbes, was informed with a moral

8. HD, x, 147.
9. For a more extended comparison of Swift and Auden, see the recent article by Monroe K. Spears, "Late Auden: The Satirist as Lunatic Clergyman," *Sewanee Review,* 59 (1951), 50–74.

view: it tested man's capabilities of attaining truth and goodness only after exploring the dangers which beset him at every turn. In a sense, as Leo Strauss has pointed out,[1] all of Hobbes' natural history of man was a vehicle for expressing horror at man's boundless vanity, the desire to be foremost rather than merely secure. Thus the very creation of types, in the character writing of the Overbury group or of Earle or Butler, was an implicit judgment of man as an inharmonious blend of his several humors. To invoke a type was to indicate a weakness.

The most obvious indications of such a weakness were party labels, whether literally political or drawn from the commonwealth of learning. The emergence of parties disturbed all men of Swift's age.[2] Corresponding to the assumption of the party label is the rejection of it in the man who would appear impartial and honest. Thus we find such periodical titles as *Spectator, Examiner, Plain Dealer, Guardian,* and *Common Sense* or others which deliberately assume an idiosyncrasy but at least with the air of honestly recognizing it (and thus implying that it is one that can be honorably acknowledged), such as *Grumbler, Tatler,* or *Humourist.*[3] With such guises as these, the essayist can indicate detachment and cultivate an air of impartial judgment, either an Olympian view from above the conflict or the humble view of the third person holding two opponents' coats. Where the guise is fully exploited, it leads almost invariably to a comic view of the subject, from which the passions of others seem pointless or exaggerated and their actions can be separated from plausible motives.

Clearly enough, the detached spectator himself might become a questionable type, for as Matthew Prior wrote, "our Mind is such a buissy thing that it will never stand Neuter, but is medling and interesting it self upon all Occasions . . . We cannot see two People play but we take part with one, and wish the other should lose, this without any previous reason or consideration." [4] This inevitability of some partisan spirit gives ironic point to the author's account of himself in the *Battle of the Books:* "I, being possessed of all Qualifications requisite in an *Historian,* and retained by neither Party; have resolved to comply with

1. Leo Strauss, *The Political Philosophy of Hobbes: Its Basis and Its Genesis,* tr. Elsa M. Sinclair (Oxford, Clarendon Press, 1936), pp. 6–29.

2. "I remember some Time ago in one of the *'Tatlers,'* to have read a Letter, wherein several Reasons are assigned for the present Corruption and Degeneracy of our Taste; but I think the Writer hath omitted the principal One, which I take to be the Prejudice of Parties." *Examiner,* No. 19 (14 December 1710), HD, III, 35 (TS, IX, 114).

3. Cf. James Sutherland, "Some Aspects of Eighteenth-Century Prose," *Essays on the Eighteenth Century: Presented to David Nichol Smith* (Oxford, Clarendon Press, 1945), p. 99. See also Harold D. Kelling, *"Gulliver's Travels:* A Comedy of Humours," *University of Toronto Quarterly, 21* (1952), 362–75, esp. 362–5.

4. Matthew Prior, "An Essay upon Opinion," *Dialogues of the Dead and Other Works in Prose and Verse,* ed. A. R. Waller (Cambridge, Cambridge University Press, 1907), p. 200.

the urgent *Importunity of my Friends,* by writing down a full impartia. Account thereof." [5] Not only does the author blindly assert omnicompetence and a disinterested motive, he assumes as well the possibility of easy impartiality. Swift, in contrast, allowed himself only the playful assertion to Archbishop King that he was "a strict examiner, and a very good judge." In his recommendation of a man to the younger Harley he shows the standard of rational expectation. "He is prudent enough to comply with the times," Swift wrote, "which I know not how he could well avoid without a virtue too transcendent for this age. Yet I do not hear any marks of his violence in party affairs." Somewhere, then, between the violence of party spirit and a complete transcendence of it lay the possible mean; the first extreme was all too possible, the second scarcely so and usually professed only by the hypocrite or dunce. The mask of impartiality, if it were not qualified by humor, was as much a questionable type as were those of partisan zeal. Constant claims of "modest proposals" to "universal benefit" were keys to pretentious and specious disinterestedness. "I burnt all my Lord ——'s letters," Swift wrote to Betty Germain, "upon receiving one where he had used these words to me, 'all I pretend to is a great deal of sincerity,' which indeed, was the chief virtue he wanted." [6]

The central issue was the primary Augustan one of interest; no other ethical question so clearly revealed the conflict of reason and imagination. The truly rational man would see that his interest was the same as that of the whole society; the knave would pretend to serve the common interest while he pursued his own; the fool would mistake his own or his leader's interest for that of society. Self-knowledge was necessary to prevent self-deception or deception by others. If one did not wish to be a knave, one had also to avoid becoming the tool of knaves:

knavish men are fitter to deal with others of their own denomination; while those who are honest and best-intentioned may be the instruments of as much mischief to the public, for want of cunning, as the greatest knaves; and more, because of the charitable opinion which they are apt to have of others. Therefore, how to join the prudence of the serpent with the innocency of the dove, in this affair, is the most difficult point. It is not so hard to find an honest man, as to make this honest man active, and vigilant, and skilful; which, I doubt, will re-

5. HD, 1, 145 (TS, 1, 165).

6. *Correspondence,* 1, 68 (Swift to King, 1 January 1707/8); v, 85 (Swift to Harley, 30 August 1734); v, 186 (Swift to Lady Betty Germain, 8 June 1735). Cf. a lighter version of this complaint: "I am sorry to find a lady make use of the word paradise, from which you turned us out as well as yourselves; and pray tell me freely how many of your sex bring it along with them to their husbands' houses?" *Correspondence,* v, 300 (Swift to Mrs. Pendarves, 29 January 1735/6).

ur of profit greater than my scheme will afford him, unless
e contented with the honour of serving his country, and the
f a good conscience.[7]

The rhetorical end Swift typically sets himself is teaching men to distinguish their true interest from plausible deceptions. In *The Conduct
of the Allies* he appeals to all, "whether *Whig* or *Tory,* whose private Interest is best answered by the Welfare of their Country." As the Drapier
he insists upon the "common or general interest" of the Irish people.
Nor could vigilance be left to the expert. Addison wrote in the *Free-
Holder:* "It is the duty of an honest and prudent man, to sacrifice a doubtful opinion to the concurring judgement of those whom he believes to be
well intentioned to their country, and who have better opportunities of
looking into all its most complicated interests." We have Swift's marginal
comment: "A motion to make men go every length with their party. I
am sorry to see such a principle in this author." [8]

We have seen the ironic mask emerging as the means of giving coherence to moral solecisms, as the methodizing of wit. From the other direction we can see the statement of interest assuming the qualities of an
ironic mask, as the statement shifts from direct presentation of a sound
ethos to the indirect suggestion of it through the distortions of a fool or
a knave. The very difficulty of defining true interest with precision encourages a method of witty indirection.

In order to be read at all, irony must be read critically; the reader must
supply the good sense that the speaker lacks and that the reader himself
has too often failed to exercise. To this extent irony, like wit, is a trap. In
wit the reader is led by the ease of sophistry into a startling revaluation,
in irony by the familiarity of tone into unpleasant recognition and often
revulsion. In the nonironic works this familiarity of tone is the necessary
shared agreement of speaker and audience; the speaker's moral sensibility
must appeal to the audience and win its confidence. We can see the movement toward irony in the different uses Swift makes of this confidence.

The Sentiments of a Church of England Man is almost a tour de force
in its utter resistance of party views. The title proclaims a clear allegiance
and defined interest. This definition is important in discussion of public
affairs, "where the most inconsiderable have some *real* Share, and by
the wonderful Importance which every Man is of to himself, a very
great *imaginary* one." So long, Swift holds, as there is not yet a state
of war in which no man is neutral, one may still hope to moderate between extremes and define an interest which is fully represented by neither
party. "In consequence of this free Use of my Reason, I cannot possibly

7. *A Letter on Mr. McCulla's Project about Halfpence,* TS, VII, 188.
8. HD, VI, 45 (TS, V, 103); HD, X, 3 (TS, VI, 13); TS, X, 374–5 (Addison, *Free-
Holder,* No. 29 [30 March 1716]).

think so well or so ill of either Party, as they would endeavour to per-
suade the World of each other, and of themselves." [9] We might expect
"as they think of each other," but Swift has more to say, and his cheating
of expectation heightens his point. The views of partisans are found not
in a search for truth but in a search for rhetorical weapons. They may
come to believe what they say, but they say what they want the world
to believe. The Church of England Man offers his sentiments, therefore,
"in such a Manner as may not be liable to least Objection from either
Party, and which I am confident would be assented to by great Numbers
in both, if they were not misled to those mutual Misrepresentations, by
such Motives as they would be ashamed to own." Even when a midpoint must be chosen between the two views and thus both must be accepted in some measure, each is given its special value at the expense of
the other:

> Now, because it is a Point of Difficulty to chuse an exact middle be-
> tween two ill Extreams; it may be worth enquiring in the present Case,
> which of these a wise and good Man would rather seem to avoid: Tak-
> ing therefore their own good and ill Characters with due Abatements
> and Allowances for Partiality and Passion; I should think that, in
> order to preserve the Constitution entire in Church and State; who-
> ever hath a true Value for both, would be sure to avoid the Extreams
> of *Whig* for the Sake of the former, and the Extreams of Tory on Ac-
> count of the latter.

Swift by this method is able to frustrate any impulses one might feel to
depend upon a partisan leader. One cannot resign clear knowledge of
true interest and the free use of reason by which it is obtained. Moderation between extreme views, the Church of England Man recognizes, is
of all the programs "the least consistent with the common Design, of making a Fortune by the *Merit* of an *Opinion*." The very circumspection of
the Church of England Man, the modesty of his own claims, and the real-
ism with which he views others' make his attitudes highly acceptable.
He has seen all one might expect; there are no blind spots, no solecisms.[1]

In the figure of the Drapier, Swift comes closer to full use of the ironic
speaker. In the first place, the characterization is richer. The Drapier
can assert his honesty and respectability, for he is "no inconsiderable
Shop-Keeper"; on the other hand, he can understand only what is evident to a "poor ignorant Shop-Keeper," unschooled in refinements.[2]
Swift was aware that many of the Irish were too degraded by poverty
to see their own interest clearly: "I live in a nation of slaves, who sell

9. HD, ii, 2 (TS, iii, 51–2).
1. HD, ii, 2, 24–5, 2 (TS, iii, 54, 75, 52).
2. HD, x, 16, 29 (TS, vi, 34, 64).

themselves for nothing." [3] In the Drapier he created a man prosperous enough to resist temptation but enough an Irishman to identify his interests with the kingdom's. The Drapier's praise of the jurors who failed to find against him serves to explain his own merit as well: "as Philosophers say, *Vertue is seated in the Middle;* so in another Sense, the little *Virtue* left in the World is chiefly to be found among the *middle* Rank of Mankind; who are neither *allured* out of her Paths by *Ambition,* nor *driven* by Poverty." [4] Ireland must suffer its large property owners to live abroad on the wealth they draw from their country; the Drapier, as a tradesman, is bound to his nation by the very limits of his means. So far he is a direct speaker with a clear interest.

Insofar, however, as the Drapier wishes to accept the dictates of the English or to assent to their self-justification, he becomes an ironic speaker. When he is unable to conform, he recognizes that he may be charged with being *"Pragmatical* and *Overweening"* or "more speculative than others of [his] Condition." His defense is the typical one of the satirist, the greatness of his provocation: "It is a known Story of the Dumb Boy, whose Tongue forced a Passage for Speech by the Horror of seeing a Dagger at his Father's Throat. This may lessen the Wonder, that a Tradesman hid in Privacy and Silence should *cry out* when the Life and Being of his Political *Mother* are attempted before his Face; and by so infamous a Hand." But this declaration of the limits of endurance gives way to apparent compliance, to the need to consider "the *Climate* I was in." He promises to bury "at the Bottom of a strong Chest" all the books he owns "that treat of *Liberty;* and [to] spread over a *Layer* or two of *Hobbs, Filmer,* [and] *Bodin.*"

> But, if your Lordship will please to give me an easy Lease of some Part of your Estate in *Yorkshire,* thither I will carry my Chest; and turning it upside down, resume my political Reading where I left it off; feed on plain homely Fare, and live and die a FREE honest *English* Farmer.[5]

The figure of the chest allows the Drapier to turn compliance into a simple inversion of normal values. The Drapier, then, must play the projector in opposing injustice; in his "normal" conformity he must overturn all that men should value. In the definition of his own interest, the Drapier is not unlike the Church of England Man; he becomes an ironic speaker at the point that he professedly sees his resistance with the eyes of the English.

In the *Argument against Abolishing Christianity* a third level of meaning is introduced. The author of the *Argument* occupies a middle ground: he accepts the general ends of his age but differs with most people about

3. *Correspondence,* v, 143 (Swift to Pulteney, 8 March 1734/5).
4. HD, x, 90 (TS, vi, 171–2).
5. HD, x, 81–2, 90, 93–4 (TS, vi, 170, 175, 176).

the choice of means. He agrees that Christianity is meaningless but denies that its forms are valueless; in his terms, he joins with his contemporaries in discarding "real Christianity" but wishes in opposition to preserve "nominal Christianity." The central contrast of the pamphlet is between God and Mammon, a true Christian faith and "our present Schemes of Wealth and Power." The author tries to introduce a third term, a reconciliation of the two. He shows that nominal Christianity does nothing to inhibit "those Methods most in Use towards the Pursuit of Greatness, Riches, and Pleasure" and that, instead, it can be made to serve them well by providing a harmless diversion. Christianity is like a tub cast out to keep the whale from attacking the ship of state; one must consider "what an Advantage and Felicity it is, for great Wits to be always provided with Objects of Scorn and Contempt, in order to exercise and improve their Talents, and divert their Spleen from falling on each other, or on themselves." [6]

Before the author can present his argument, he must apologize for his resistance to the abolishing of Christianity: "I know not how, whether from the Affectation of Singularity, or the Perverseness of human Nature; but so it unhappily falls out, that I cannot be entirely of [the common] Opinion." Like the Drapier he can venture no positive opposition to the popular or official view, but the ironic contrast between his own view and the view to which he submits is not so simple as in the case of the Drapier. In effecting his reconciliation, he strips Christianity of all meaning: "If the Quiet of a State can be bought by only flinging Men a few Ceremonies to devour, it is a Purchase no wise Man would refuse." [7] The attempt to save the name of Christianity generates the kind of situation which inevitably produces cant. Once words have lost their meaning they may serve any end. Here the author is interested only in showing how ineffectual the original meaning will be. He is not himself deceived by such cant, but he describes the situation in which most men would be. The position of the author becomes one of comic simplicity: it avoids both the need to attend to Christian teaching and the need to take action against it. He can look with some disdain at those who take Christianity seriously enough to want to abolish it. They cannot see that it is merely a system of forms, of no real disadvantage and even useful in providing the moral equivalent of factionalism. He can point to the waste motion of a plan to abolish Christianity and pride himself on accomplishing equivalent ends with greater economy and even incidental advantages.

The author is so far from professing concern with the true meaning of Christianity that he hardly seems a victim of moral confusion. His obliviousness to moral problems and his commitment to the ends of

6. HD, II, 28, 33, 35–6 (TS, III, 7, 13, 16).
7. HD, II, 26, 35 (TS, III, 5, 15–16).

"Wealth and Power" free him of any real responsibility. He is a step beyond the majority of men in not trying to sustain a hypocritical profession, and he can systematize all the more effectively the conversion of a doctrine of restraint into a mask of interest. Although the words which enjoin this restraint have become meaningless in use, they still carry meanings which are dangerously capable of being reinvigorated. When the author accedes to the popular will to abolish Christianity, therefore, he warns of the need to abolish all notions of religion:

> For, as long as we leave in Being a God and his Providence, with all the necessary Consequences, which curious and inquisitive Men will be apt to draw from such Premises; we do not strike at the Root of the Evil, though we should ever so effectually annihilate the present Scheme of the Gospel. For, of what Use is Freedom of Thought, if it will not produce Freedom of Action; which is the sole End, how remote soever, in Appearance, of all Objections against Christianity? [8]

In the author of the *Argument,* as in the Drapier giving his account of the chest of books, we can see the careful acceptance of the world's values as genuine, the grave entertainment of a specious view for the sake of exposing it. This is typically the method of irony, but there are many versions of the method. The Drapier can make his point neatly in the reversal of the chest; the author of the *Argument* presses gradually to the disclosure of the interest which makes a cloak of any doctrine and can change its doctrine as vogues demand.

In each of the three cases we have considered, the author is given a character which allows the work to use certain rhetorical techniques. The Church of England Man has a fixed position outside the range of party contentions; he can see both the full range and the desirable midpoint more easily than the active partisan. He is, to an extent, the Persian or Chinese visitor to party conflicts, but since he has a stake in them as well he can present the conscious deliberation of the man who must decide between counterclaims. The Drapier is also a man whose interest is at stake and is clearly defined; he is free of delusions of "imaginary importance" and also of dull submission. His limited education makes him incapable of following refinements of political doctrine; he reduces every term to strict meaningfulness and thereby strips Power of its obscure pretension to Right. When he does profess submission, the irony is sharp and the reversal clear. Finally, the author of the *Argument* is more clear sighted than those he opposes, but he is superior only as a technician. He accepts their false ends, only to demonstrate how readily they are obtained through corruption rather than violence, and he makes clear how completely our ends may be reversed with no change in sur-

8. HD, ii, 37–8 (TS, iii, 18–19).

face forms or in names. All three of the authors make cant untenable, but
they do it in increasing degrees of indirectness and of apparent compliance.

A MODEST PROPOSAL

In *A Modest Proposal* Swift achieves the most economical and intense
use of the ironic mask. The apparent author is an ingenious projector
attempting what no one before has achieved, a reconciliation of England's interest with Ireland's and a demonstration that in Ireland, as well
as in other lands, people are the riches of a nation. Recent scholars have
shown that the Modest Proposer is not only a typical projector but, more
important, a typical theorist of a certain kind, the political arithmetician.
The burden of the satire may be taken to rest upon the economic theorists
of the day—men like Petty, Petyt, Child, Brewster, and Defoe—or upon
the conditions which make their theories inapplicable to Ireland.

In effect, Swift is maintaining that the maxim—people are the riches
of a nation—applies to Ireland only if Ireland is permitted slavery or
cannibalism. The terrible irony in the bare maxim, divested of
its supporting arguments, was even more apparent at this time than
usual because of the famine conditions which prevailed in Ireland after
three successive failures in harvests.[9]

What we have is a paradoxical application of the maxim to Ireland written in a style which betrays no awareness of the paradox and which resembles very closely the scientific manner of the economic projectors of the
day.

As in the poetic fables or in Gulliver's initial account of the "very short
and soft" grass of Lilliput, Swift prepares unobtrusively for the surprise
which follows. The very first paragraph shows the displacement of tone
which characterizes the author's insensibility:

It is a melancholy object to those, who walk through this great town,
or travel in the country, when they see the streets, the roads, and cabin-
doors, crowded with beggars of the female sex, followed by three, four,
or six children, *all in rags,* and importuning every passenger for an
alms. These mothers instead of being able to work for their honest livelihood, are forced to employ all their time in strolling, to beg sustenance

9. Louis A. Landa, *"A Modest Proposal* and Populousness," *Modern Philology,* 40
(1942), 162, 165. See also George Wittkowsky, "Swift's *Modest Proposal:* The Biog-
raphy of an Early Georgian Pamphlet," *Journal of the History of Ideas,* 4 (1943),
65–104, esp. 94–5; Louis A. Landa, "Swift's Economic Views and Mercantilism," *ELH,*
10 (1943), 310–35; Cleanth Brooks, *Modern Poetry and the Tradition* (Chapel Hill,
University of North Carolina Press, 1939), pp. 226–7.

> for their helpless infants, who, as they grow up, either turn thieves for
> want of work, or leave their dear Native Country to fight for the Pre-
> tender in Spain, or sell themselves to the Barbadoes.[1]

There is a certain fastidious preciseness of phrase in this which belies
the sympathy one might expect. The reaction of the author to the beggars
is clearly that of the passing observer, and his profession of sentiment
in "melancholy" is counteracted by the classificatory interest of "beggars
of the female sex, followed by three, four, or six children." There is
no necessary conflict between genuine compassion and preciseness of
observation, the virtuoso in the world's laboratory. The strangeness
of tone becomes more apparent when the "beggars of the female sex" become "mothers" but mothers whose children render them unable "to work
for their honest livelihood." This view of motherhood is coupled with
"helpless infants," a phrase which might render conventional pity but
which here designates an encumbrance to respectable labor. Finally the
slight incongruity of "this great town" gives emphasis to the later reference to a "dear Native Country" which children must desert in order
to find a living. The play on the emptiness of stale terms is one of Swift's
favorite entertainments. Here it is characterization of an author who lives
by "refined jargon."

So far we may simply be disturbed by the author's ability to consider
human misery in detached economic terms and still to retain the stereo-
types of compassion and patriotism. In what follows, the zeal of a projector becomes apparent as well:

> whoever could find out a fair, cheap and easy method of making these
> children sound useful members of the commonwealth would deserve
> so well of the public, as to have his statue set up for a preserver of the
> nation.
>
> But my intention is very far from being confined to provide only for
> the children of professed beggars, it is of a much greater extent, and
> shall take in the whole number of infants at a certain age, who are born
> of parents in effect as little able to support them, as those who demand
> our charity in the streets.[2]

This last sentence has a multiple function. It reflects the ambition of a
projector who would outdo all rivals with a comprehensive plan when
even a more moderate aim has not yet been satisfied. It points, also,
to the full extent of Irish poverty: the cottagers no less than the beggars
demand our charity. The plan must become the more extravagant to
meet a problem so vast. The situation of Ireland (both in its poverty
and in its subjection to England's mercantile colonial policy) is such
that only a fool can hope to satisfy both justice and the English. The

1. TS, VII, 207.
2. TS, VII, 207–8.

ambition is another side of the obtuseness we have already seen. So far it is only foolish, but an ominous note is prepared in the phrasing: "sound useful members of the commonwealth," like "helpless infants" before, ironically foreshadows the proposal that is to be made. As usual, Swift is preparing his text to shift easily into a further level of meaning which will reverse the import of the whole tract.

Once the zeal of the projector is established, his moral nature is allowed to become more obvious. Mothers become "dams" and "breeders," children are "dropped." The Modest Proposer can mourn for "the poor innocent babes" murdered by their mothers; but he can look forward to making them "contribute to the feeding and partly to the clothing of many thousands." The intensity and obliviousness of his economic interest lead him to weigh the usefulness of children's proficiency in the art of theft. When the proposal is finally set forth, it is delicately qualified by a regard for refined modern tastes: "a young healthy child well nursed is at a year old a most delicious, nourishing, and wholesome food, whether stewed, roasted, baked, or boiled, *and I make no doubt that it will equally serve in a fricassee or ragout.*" [3] The use of physical horror—the plan for "buying the children alive, and dressing them hot under the Knife" —has much the same function as the use of disgust in other works. Just as man's pride in his rationality must be confronted with a concrete image of his animal drives in the Yahoos, the benign theorizers about economic man must be made to see their abstraction come to life at the very moment when their inhumanity is most flagrant. The concrete instance tests the theory: that it does not destroy it for the Modest Proposer is due to his singular blindness. That blindness, in turn, is only an exaggeration of a more common indifference, the refusal or the inability to see the concrete and the readiness to submit to noble pretensions.

The proposal is offered, not by an Englishman with the indifference of a superior foreigner but by an Irishman anxious to please England, the kind of eager collaborator who can outdo the oppressors. "Swift's anger was always divided between the stupidity of the Irish and the rapacity of the English," [4] but Irish stupidity could be something worse: "there is not a more undeserving vicious race of human kind than the bulk of those who are reduced to beggary, even as this beggarly country." [5] It is Swift's ability to see the degradation, moral as well as economic, of the victims who submit to the victors that gives universality to such a work as the *Modest Proposal.* Swift lamented that in Ireland "the blessing of increase and multiply is . . . converted into a curse: and, as marriage hath been ever countenanced in all free countries, so we should be less miserable if it were discouraged in ours, as far as can be

---

3. TS, VII, 209. Italics added.
4. *The Drapier's Letters,* ed. Davis, introd., p. xi.
5. *A Proposal for Giving Badges to the Beggars of Dublin,* TS, VII, 329-30.

consistent with Christianity." [6] In the modest proposal, marriage is made to prosper by conforming with interest:

> This would be a great inducement to marriage, which all wise nations have either encouraged by rewards, or enforced by laws and penalties. It would increase the care and tenderness of mothers toward their children, when they are sure of a settlement for life, to the poor babes, provided in some sort by the public for their annual profit instead of expense. We should see an honest emulation among the married women, which of them could bring the fattest child to the market, men would become as fond of their wives during the time of their pregnancy, as they are now of their mares in foal, their cows in calf, or sows when they are ready to farrow, nor offer to beat or kick them (as is too frequent a practice) for fear of a miscarriage.[7]

There is more general irony in this passage than in most of the tract; not only is Ireland's plight underlined and the author's grossness further exposed, but a general tendency in all men is suggested. Decent human behavior is made possible only by the coincidental demands of interest. Proper family relations are possible only as the chance appearances of real selfishness. People do not serve God; they occasionally appear to do so when the worship of Mammon requires similar gestures. This goes beyond even La Rochefoucauld: there is no hypocrisy here, no homage paid virtue by vice, only the accident of resemblance. The Modest Proposer is rationalizing not merely England's oppression but man's universal lack of charity.

The same note is struck in the final sentence: "I have no children, by which I can propose to get a single penny; the youngest being nine years old, and my wife past childbearing." [8] We can see most clearly the reason for the theorizer's detachment: he is free of facing the concrete instance himself. That he is capable of considering it is damning enough, but more is suggested. The accusations he fends off are such as might be made when men once esteem children for their commercial value and their wives as the producers of commodities. The very fullness of meaning that Swift's irony suggests saves the tract from the flatness of propaganda; the Modest Proposer implicates more and more of us in his own madness. His obtuseness becomes the comic counterpart of a much more terrible moral degradation. This device is frequent in Swift: his patient fools are always less terrible than the knaves they betray. The surface of the irony is a comedy of irresponsible folly, of the moral obliviousness of a dedicated pedant or theorist. Beneath the surface lies the guilt of most men, who are less naïve and transparent but all the more responsible.

6. TS, VII, 330.
7. TS, VII, 214.
8. TS, VII, 216.

V

The Symbolic Works

SYMBOLISM AND STRUCTURE

SYMBOLS are the concrete embodiment of relationships. In Swift's sermons and tracts, symbolic patterns often emerge at the close of an argument and fix in a pictorial or dramatic analogy the relations that have been presented abstractly. In a longer work such analogies may be used repeatedly. The sun, for example, may be turned to a number of functions: like reason, it may outlast the gaudy clouds of rhetoric; like judgment, it may govern its universe with order and proportion; like divine love, it may warm and attract all that moves about it. The suggestiveness of the sun symbol is the vast range of relations it may condense into one image; it is the task of the writer to make as many of these relations as possible relevant to his work. On the other hand, a single relationship may be given a vast range of embodiments; the balance of extremes, for example, may be evoked in the ethical mean, in the architect's balance of stresses, in the stability of the middle rank of society, in the precarious stance of man in the Great Chain of Being. The wider the range of relations a symbol may represent, or the wider the range of symbols that represent a relation, the more dense the meaning of a work and the more precisely qualified. The effect is somewhat as if the author had plotted the points through which a curve might be drawn: the relation must be general enough to satisfy each of these symbols, and, once it is abstracted, it may suggest countless new ones. The finest symbols are perhaps those that resist any neat formulation into a simple meaning; rather, they may suggest the pattern of the curve or even of several possible curves through the same points without allowing their suggestiveness to be lost in a single equation.

Swift's method in his two major works is based largely on the creation of symbolic patterns, in both cases reductive patterns. In each work this reductive pattern emerges in spite of the narrator and comes to include all that he has granted the highest dignity. To this extent, there is mere transvaluation: high becomes low. But in the course of including so much of man's behavior, these reductive patterns acquire a dignity of their own, a "bad eminence" that makes man's vice and folly a thorough and terrible inversion of his true goodness. The pressure with which

Swift reduces so many patterns of handsome corruption to those of the Bedlam inmate or the Yahoo gives weight and intensity to his simplification.

Even more, the simplification is not all that it seems. First of all, it provides a general pattern of incongruity by which meaning is given to a great range of detail. The ambitious amplification of the mock author of *A Tale of a Tub* and the ingenuous awe of Gulliver are both set off at every point by the underlying symbolic patterns of the book. Each event, each important word, is given a complexity of meaning that the author cannot discern. More important, the reductive patterns are not the whole truth. If two curves of quite different pattern can be drawn through the same points, at least a third seems possible. If we have come to see the weakness of the conventional distinction between greatness and baseness, we need not abandon either the words or the distinction but consider both anew. The eventual identification of carping and serenity (of Jack and Peter) in the *Tale* and the impossible choice of Gulliver between Houyhnhnm and Yahoo are Swift's devices for dissolving the reductive simplicity he has opposed to an uncritical complacency. A middle view is left for the reader to define.

In both *A Tale of a Tub* and *Gulliver's Travels* the symbolic pattern is freed of dependence upon abstract argument. The general meanings are implied in the pattern of event or image. In neither work is the narrative structure allowed to become so tightly coherent as to demand simple allegorical equations, although there are particular allegorical meanings among others in parts of both books. Nor, on the other hand, do Swift's symbols become vague and indefinite. The complexity lies in the conflict of rather precise patterns; in *Gulliver's Travels* the conflict is finally dramatized in the dilemma of the hero. In these works, then, we are confronted with a new situation. Instead of starting with generalities which acquire a weight of suggestion through symbolic patterns, we start almost at once with elaborate symbolic patterns and move toward apparent simplification. It is useful to compare the two works in their themes, their symbolism, and their irony. Between them they represent all of Swift's methods at their best.[1]

1. In the treatment of *A Tale of a Tub* that follows I am indebted to Émile Pons, *Swift: Les Années de jeunesse et le "Conte du Tonneau"* (Strasbourg, Librairie Istra, 1925), and to Miriam K. Starkman, *Swift's Satire on Learning in A Tale of a Tub* (Princeton, Princeton University Press, 1950). For *Gulliver's Travels* I have made considerable use of two articles: John F. Ross, "The Final Comedy of Lemuel Gulliver," *Studies in the Comic* (Berkeley, University of California Press, 1941), pp. 175–96; and Joe Horrell, "What Gulliver Knew," *Sewanee Review, 51* (1943), 476–504. Throughout I have used Ricardo Quintana, *The Mind and Art of Jonathan Swift* (London and New York, Oxford, 1936) and "Situational Satire: A Commentary on the Method of Swift," *University of Toronto Quarterly, 17* (1947), 130–6.

COMMON THEMES

The theme of inversion is one of many in Swift, but it is an important one, a peculiar concern of his age as of our own. It is difficult to read the last books of George Orwell, for example, without being frequently reminded of Swift. And it is difficult, on the other hand, to read Plato, at least with the guidance of John Wild's recent book, without seeing both Swift's problems and our own. Orwell in *Nineteen Eighty-Four* has given us a picture of a society which must create its own past and indeed its own world. In its worship of power, it claims right as well by constantly re-creating the world to justify its own acts. History must be revised at every moment, memory must be destroyed, all threat of an objective truth must be overcome. Wild's analysis of the world's present ills is similar. He finds our chief danger in "idealism," and he sees three symptoms of its prevalence: the "absence of any faith in a real order of existence, independent of the opinions and desires of the national group"; a "scorn for reason, except as the contriver of technical instruments"; and a contempt for the rational individual.[2]

Whatever one may think of this analysis of the modern situation, it could not have greatly displeased Swift. If there is a central preoccupation running through Swift's work, it is surely something very close to the theme Wild stresses in Plato—anatropism, the inversion of culture. The inversion may be the rule of the tyrant, of a man like Callicles or Thrasymachus who considers justice a mere convention imposed by power; or it may be the guidance of the sophist, who fits all moral terms "to the fancies of the great beast and calls what it enjoys good and what vexes it bad." Within the individual it is the rule of appetite, the failure "to subdue the brutish parts of our nature to the human," the willingness "to enslave our humanity to the savagery of the beast." Wild shows the fundamental importance in Plato's work of the contrast "between the true, upward way of life, and the downward way which *thinks* it is going up."[3]

In Swift the problem of inversion is stated as the threat of corruption —the barbarity which is "kept out with so much Difficulty, by so few Hands."[4] Society is constantly degenerating into forms which cease to effect control over the individual will and in fact are turned by the will to its own purposes. So, too, the men who rule the society fail in

2. John Wild, *Plato's Theory of Man: An Introduction to the Realistic Philosophy of Culture* (Cambridge, Harvard University Press, 1946), p. 2.

3. *The Republic of Plato*, tr. Francis M. Cornford (London and New York, Oxford, 1945), pp. 200, 317. Wild, *Plato's Theory of Man*, p. 38; see the whole section on "Plato's Conception of Anatrope," pp. 34–44.

4. *The History of the Four Last Years of the Queen*, HD, VII, 106 (TS, X, 126).

the virtue which alone makes them human and become instead the instruments of their own or of a party's will. Their words finally, when they lose their proper meaning, become the means of deception or domination.

In *A Tale of a Tub* Swift dramatizes the corruptions of religion and learning in two ways: the allegory embodies in the career of typical Restoration fops the history of the church in the world, and the prefaces and digressions embody in a continuous dramatic monologue the bathos and pretentious folly of the modern spirit. The monologue includes numerous symbolic accounts of the corruption of learning; they are presented as a panegyric upon the moderns, but they are written in the language of a man so obtuse and uncritical that he unwittingly betrays his case at every turn. Since Swift is concerned with the misuse of religion to serve "schemes of wealth and power," his allegory treats religion on the level of manners, as one more means of achieving self-aggrandizement or domination at the expense of reason. True religion can survive only if man serves God; when man serves himself and seeks "sublunary happiness" as an end in itself, as Swift frequently points out, he may use *nominal* Christianity as an instrument, but he has already discarded true Christianity. The three brothers of the allegory slay "certain Dragons" but soon come to the town, the *grand monde* or world of fashion. They cease, in short, to redeem the time but live for it instead, and fashion becomes Swift's principal symbol of this absorption in the world.

Much of the *Tale* is built around the contrast of the temporal or fashionable and the permanent or timeless. The Epistle to Prince Posterity first shows the inevitable conflict of Time and the ambitions of a time-bound generation. The moderns seek distinction rather than truth, and they seek it by novelty and singularity, by ignoring the universal or enduring. Though they seek to reach Posterity by evading the judgment of Time, their works vanish before they can so much as offer them. In seeking distinction, the moderns wish to *conquer* the past. "I here think fit," says the Tale Teller, "to lay hold on that great and honourable Privilege of being the *Last Writer;* I claim an absolute Authority in Right, as the *freshest Modern,* which gives me a Despotick Power over all Authors before me." [5] The result of this view is self-indulgence—private meaning, "tender wit," ephemeral achievement. The Tale Teller's demonstration of his own age's greatness collapses, and he is finally left clinging to the specious present: "what I am going to say is literally true this Minute I am writing." [6]

What is ephemeral, however, may be praised all the more as fashionable, and Swift uses clothes symbolism to present this inversion. The three coats of the brothers (the simple and plain truths of doctrine) become, in their misuse, the instruments of pride and worldly ambition.

5. HD, i, 81 (TS, i, 94).
6. HD, i, 22 (TS, i, 37).

The Tale Teller is ready to systematize this, and he presents us with an inverted theology to support inverted practices and institutions. The God of the clothes philosophy is the tailor, who "daily create[s] Men, by a kind of Manufactory Operation." His creatures, which "the World calls improperly *Suits of Cloaths,*" are "in Reality the most refined Species of Animals"—in fact, "Rational Creatures, or Men." The soul of man is really his celestial or outer suit, daily created anew, and its faculties are parts of dress:

> *Embroidery,* was *Sheer wit; Gold Fringe* was *agreeable Conversation,* Gold Lace was Repartee, a huge long *Periwig* was *Humour,* and a *Coat full of Powder* was very good *Raillery:* All which required abundance of *Finesse* and *Delicatesse* to manage with Advantage, as well as strict Observance after Times and Fashions.

The implications are clear: when the end of man is self-love and distinction and his means singularity or fashion, he has no standards which endure, no integrity. In a sense, he has ceased to have a soul at all, for when religion and the soul cease to be regulatory and moral they have become lackeys rather than masters and no longer deserve their original names: "Is not Religion a *Cloak,* Honesty a *Pair of Shoes,* worn out in the Dirt, Self-love a *Surtout,* Vanity a *Shirt,* and Conscience a *Pair of Breeches,* which, tho' a Cover for Lewdness as well as Nastiness, is easily slipt down for the Service of both." [7]

Elsewhere, Swift deals at length with the instability of happiness as a human end. The pagan philosophers, never able to agree about the *summum bonum,* either became cynical skeptics or, for lack of any solid faith, were inclined "to fall into the vulgar pursuits of common men, to hunt after greatness and riches, to make their court, and to serve occasions." The world offers no stable end; only heavenly wisdom ("a daily vision of God") can provide it.[8] To return to the words of the *Tale,* "as human Happiness is of a very short Duration, so in those Days were human Fashions, upon which it entirely depends." [9] The very nature of fashion makes every victory a necessary defeat. The pattern of natural man for Swift, as for Hobbes, shows him endlessly acquisitive and endlessly unsatisfied.[1] Such limited self-love involves the need for superiority or pre-eminence; at best it retains the spirit of opposition, the love of party or sect. Reason seeks victory instead of truth and becomes sophistry in the process. Knowledge gives way to an imagination which can frame a gratifying image of the world. The soul itself becomes a mere image of

---

7. HD, i, 46–8 (TS, i, 61–3).
8. *On the Wisdom of This World,* HD, ix, 244, 248 (TS, iv, 175, 178).
9. HD, i, 51 (TS, i, 65).
1. "For learning, like all true merit, is easily satisfied; while the false and counterfeit is perpetually craving, and never thinks it has enough." TS, xi, 20.

the fashions of the day, an ever-changing garment of the body whose needs it now serves. Over all this, as Swift wrote elsewhere, hovers the threat of Time, the instrument of judgment: "Principles, as the world goes, are little more than fashion; and the apostle tells us, that 'the fashion of this world passeth away.' " [2]

The *Tale* points throughout to a middle way that lies between opposed forms of corruption. Reason is always a balance between extremes of refinement and superficiality or, as we might put it, idle curiosity and naïve credulity. Refinement takes the form of theorizing, of finding at any expense meanings which can be built into a system. It is the typical sevententh-century crime of wresting Scriptures carried into the realms of criticism, science, and philosophy. The piety of the Tale Teller requires that the hacks of Grub Street be revealed as *"Grubaean* Sages," their works as "Vehicles of Types and Fables" containing the "most finished and refined Systems of all Science and Arts." But the systems can only be revealed by "Untwisting or Unwinding"; much industry is required to force impressive meaning from trivialities. [3]

The systems themselves are either built, like "Edifices in the Air" out of sight and hearing, completely beyond empirical test, or they may be turned into "Oratorial Machines," devices for raising demagogues to a position from which they may dominate the crowd. So, too, the three ladies who lead the brothers away from simplicity are "at the very Top of the Fashion." In both cases height is the departure from the common forms which confers distinction and authority. Each system builder seeks to conquer all of nature, as do the moderns all of literature, and thereby to overthrow all rival systems. The Tale Teller boasts of an essay on the number three: "I have by most convincing Proofs, not only reduced the *Senses* and the *Elements* under its Banner, but brought over several Deserters from its two great Rivals *SEVEN* and *NINE*." [4] The system builder becomes, in short, the hero in the universe of fashion. Swift places together all revolutions "in empire, philosophy, and religion." Each is achieved by the conqueror's reduction of "Multitudes to his own *Power,* his *Reasons* or his *Visions*." [5] The patterns of conqueror, bully, and tyrant all contribute to the archetype by which proselytizing and system building are to be understood. In his account of Bedlam Swift finally shows the fundamental standard of this inverted world; madness is only heroism out of fashion.

The story of the three brothers is itself one of the typical modern systems, a reductive allegory of the history of the church from its primi-

2. "Advertisement to the Reader," *Memoirs of Captain John Creichton,* TS, XI, 167. Cf. I *Corinthians* 7 : 31.
3. HD, I, 40 (TS, I, 55).
4. HD, I, 33–5 (TS, I, 48–9).
5. HD, I, 108 (TS, I, 118).

tive simplicity to its division and further corruption under the pretense of reformation and counterreformation. The story, however, is more than allegory; it provides a causal explanation of these corruptions in terms of personal morality. It allows Swift to study the individual motives which underlie the decay of religion, while the Tale Teller presents specious rationalization for a comparable decay in learning. Swift reduces the behavior of the churches to that of fops and gallants, while the Tale Teller refines foppery and gallantry into a mock religion.

The culmination of Swift's satiric point comes with the reduction of man to mechanism. Swift once noted that "climbing is performed in the same Posture with Creeping." [6] In the same way pretension which seeks to lift man above reason can also reduce him to the mechanism of physical causation. Man loses freedom when he surrenders the power of *rational* choice, and his visions have a way of turning out to be irrational compulsions. This is best illustrated in the fate of words: as sound replaces meaning and words are "spiritualized and refined . . . from the Dross and Grossness of Sense and Human Reason," their operation may be described in "physico-logical" terms. Words become weapons rather than symbols; they are "Bodies of much Weight and Gravity, as it is manifest from those deep *Impressions* they make and leave upon us; and therefore must be delivered from a due Altitude, or else they will neither carry a good Aim, nor fall down with a sufficient Force." [7] When words are reduced to mere forceful sound, all sound becomes operative. The uncritical audience which abandons a standard of rational communication treasures all forms of expression or stimulation. "For, the *Spirit* being the same in all, it is of no Import through what Vehicle it is convey'd." And Swift, in *The Mechanical Operation of the Spirit,* provides a picture of that preromantic personality, the evangelistic preacher of the Puritans: "A Master Work-man shall *blow his Nose so powerfully,* as to pierce the Hearts of his People, who are disposed to receive the *Excrements* of his Brain with the same Reverence, as the *Issue* of it. Hawking, Spitting, and Belching, the Defects of other Mens Rhetorick, are the Flowers, and Figures, and Ornaments of his." [8]

Again, the Tale Teller readily systematizes the doctrine of the Aeolists, who value inspiration and take all eccentricity to be divine possession. Their "inspiration" is literalized to the point where they affirm "the Gift of BELCHING to be the noblest Act of a Rational Creature." [9] The Aeolists do not disclaim rationality but simply invert its meaning, just as the moderns do not dismiss religion but turn it into the worship of fashion.

6. *Thoughts on Various Subjects,* HD, I, 245 (TS, I, 277).
7. HD, I, 37, 36 (TS, I, 52, 51).
8. HD, I, 183 (TS, I, 203).
9. HD, I, 96 (TS, I, 107).

Swift makes Aeolism a substitution both of the physical for the truly rational and of self-induced disease for normal health. His scheme may be reduced to a matrix somewhat as follows:

CORRUPTION		DECENCY	
Principle	*Expression*	*Expression*	*Principle*
passion	flatulency	health	reason
display	belching	speech	communication
imagination	cant	meaning	thought
domination	sound	argument	persuasion

This scheme could be extended in several ways—for example, the kinds of effect achieved in each case, conviction or ecstasy, comprehension or titillation.[1]

Reason may be neglected by the bestial Aeolists or transcended by the sophistical system builders. Swift brings the two groups together in his digression on madness. The vapors of the brain are fed by the lower parts of the body: "Mists arise from the Earth, Steams from Dunghills, Exhalations from the Sea, and Smoak from Fire; yet all Clouds are the same in Composition, as well as Consequences: and the Fumes issuing from a Jakes, will furnish as comely and useful a Vapor, as Incense from an Altar . . . [The vapors may be repressed sexuality, the rains a bursting storm of conquest.] The same Spirits, which in their superior Progress would conquer a Kingdom, descending upon the *Anus,* conclude in a *Fistula.*"[2] Higher and lower become transposed terms in this inverted world; the physical expression is at least less harmful than the spiritual. Both forms of expression are escapes from rational control, and all their issue in human conduct is an inversion of rational order, whether social or religious, poetic or rhetorical. In place of order man enjoys the endless whirl of fashion and the endless competition for distinction and power.

In *Gulliver's Travels* the same themes arise. They are not made fully explicit until the fourth voyage, but the whole book moves toward the final definition of man's nature. Only after the first three voyages have shown man's potential order and his actual disorder can Swift divide the rational aspect from the bestial. The Houyhnhnms are all order and reason, their only emotions the social or rational ones of friendship and benevolence; the Yahoos are all disorder and passion, competitive beasts vying for satisfaction and supremacy. In the scheme of the fourth voyage there is no third kind of creature—except Gulliver himself, who can no

1. For the use of a matrix, see Scott Buchanan, *Symbolic Distance in Relation to Analogy and Fiction* (London, Psyche Miniatures, 1932).
2. HD, I, 102, 104 (TS, I, 113, 115).

longer bear to see what he really is—and to one of these two must be assigned the achievements upon which civilized man prides himself. The Yahoos provide Swift countless metaphors for human institutions which have grown corrupt and inverted.

These metaphors grow out of a framework of interpretation. Swift prepares us with sufficient implicit analysis of human corruption to make the final analogies possible. Two patterns are traced throughout the earlier voyages, the meanness of man's mind and the grossness of his body.

Gulliver fails to draw any connection between the physical grossness of man and his moral nature. He neglects to see that although the Brobdingnagians reveal the horror of the human animal they also exemplify the restraint of the animal by decency and reason. Swift's pattern in these books becomes clear if we look ahead to the Yahoos, in whom physical grossness and unchecked passion are combined. Decency serves as a partial corrective of human corruption; conscience is in this sense not "a Cover for Lewdness as well as Nastiness" but a restraint upon them. This accounts for Swift's constant emphasis, in the *Tale* and in the *Travels,* upon manners; Jack's refusal "to eat his Victuals like a Christian" is a rejection of the common forms in which reason finds its compromise with man's animality. Self-indulgence and filth are virtually equated.

In the third voyage Swift closes in upon the proudest achievements of man, reducing them to the very denial of a rational nature. In Laputa, he brings together speculation, pride, foppery, and conquest. Laputa, like Lilliput, is a small and ingenious power dominating a vastly larger one. The speculative mind, like that of the system builder, demands adherence; the king, in fact, "would be the most absolute Prince in the Universe." The divorce between the distracted mind and the animal body is elaborated in the division of the Laputan family into oblivious husband and incorrigibly adulterous wife. The Flying Island (whose adamantine bottom recalls the royal prerogative with which Swift had been so much concerned in the *Drapier's Letters*) is a world of pure self-indulgence, but it is also an instrument of power sought for its own sake.

In Balnibarbi below, power is sought in the name of social improvement. The earth-bound disciples of the Laputans are, like the Aeolists of the *Tale,* "full of Volatile Spirits acquired in that Airy Region." Like the moderns of the *Tale,* they seek to attain permanence in haste and with ease: "A Palace may be built in a Week, of Materials so durable as to last for ever without repairing." [3] While Lord Munodi tries to hold on to the living past, which is the universally sound, the Balnibarbians sacrifice all to the pride which they project into a utopian future. The projectors of Lagado seek to outdo nature at any cost; art must be shown not in perfecting nature but in confounding her. Mechanical operation is

3. HD, xi, 160-1 (TS, viii, 184).

once more introduced as the escape from reason: the "laborious" method of attaining knowledge is evaded by the swallowing of wafers.[4]

The remainder of the third voyage extends and intensifies the attack upon man's achievements. First, Swift turns to man's legends of himself. The conversations with the dead leave Gulliver with a sextumvirate not of conquerors but of "Destroyers of Tyrants and Usurpers, and . . . Restorers of Liberty to oppressed and injured Nations." The truly learned are winnowed from the multitude of pedants, the few deserving from the host of corrupt and successful. Intellectual systems are seen to be, as in the *Tale,* "Fashions, which . . . vary in every Age." Finally, the price of wealth and power is shown to be the surrender of virtue and liberty: "that positive, confident, restive Temper, which Virtue infused into Man, was a perpetual Clog to publick Business." Associated with moral corruption are the loss of simplicity of "Manners, Dyet and Dress" and the growth of disease, notably the pox. The condition of the body is an index to the moral estate of man.[5]

As if in confirmation of all that Gulliver has seen at Glubbdubdrib, the court of Luggnagg reproduces once more the pomp, tyranny, and pride of man. Here the creeping of courtiers, as in Lilliput, is made literal; it is now accompanied by the licking of dust, often poisoned at the whim of the king. The "Ceremony" which Gulliver craved in Brobdingnag here overwhelms him; "a Party of Ten Horse" is sent for conducting him and his "Retinue" (one "poor Lad") to the court. But as always Gulliver is the devotee of appearance; he is altogether uncritical of the king's poisoned dust:

> I myself heard him give Directions, that one of his Pages should be whipt, whose Turn it was to give Notice about washing the Floor after an Execution, but maliciously had omitted it; by which Neglect a young Lord of great Hopes coming to an Audience, was unfortunately poisoned, although the King at that Time had no Design against his Life. But this good Prince was so gracious, as to forgive the poor Page his Whipping, upon Promise that he would do so no more, without special Orders.[6]

Gulliver is able to recognize immorality only when it is divorced from power and authority. The tyrant's expediency is equated with justice, his indifference with clemency.

The Struldbruggs provide the occasion for Swift to sum up all the forms of worldly aspiration: wealth, learning, historical wisdom. In each of these, given immortal life, Gulliver would wish to become supreme. By teaching and example he would prevent the "continual Degeneracy of

4. HD, xi, 166–8 (TS, viii, 190).
5. HD, xi, 180, 182, 184, 185 (TS, viii, 205, 207, 209, 211).
6. HD, xi, 188–9 (TS, viii, 213–14).

human Nature," but he has naïve confidence in his own ability to achieve greatness without corruption. His conviction that man can be changed by history or example, or that with the gift of immortality man can achieve virtual perfection, is the dream of "sublunary Happiness," as he calls it, given free range. All that Gulliver has neglected he sees in the actual Struldbruggs, who embody in their endless lives the whole range of human corruption. "Envy and impotent Desires, are their prevailing Passions," and these passions govern hideously decayed bodies. In Gulliver's last remarks about the Struldbruggs he has come to defend the restraints placed upon them: "Otherwise, as Avarice is the necessary Consequent of old Age, those Immortals would in time become Proprietors of the whole Nation, and engross the Civil Power; which, for want of Abilities to manage, must end in the Ruin of the Publick." [7]

Here, then, is man's unlimited corruption, at once both physical and moral, and we need not look beyond Swift's own writings to find its obvious theological explanation. In a letter written about ten years later Swift composed an allegory about his "copyhold tenure" on a "poor little house of clay":

> For the first thirty years of my life I am to pay nothing, only to do suit and service, and attend upon the courts, that are kept once a week or oftener. Four years after that I am to pay a rose every year, and farther than this, during the remainder of my life I am to pay a tooth . . . every two or three years, or oftener, if it be demanded; and when I have nothing else to pay, out with me is the word, and I will not be long before my person will be seized. I might have had my lease on much better terms, if it had not been the fault of my great-grandfather. He and his wife, with the advice of a bad neighbour, robbed an orchard belonging to the Lord of the Manor, and so forfeited their grand privileges; to my sorrow I am sure, but, however, I must do as well as I can. [8]

The movement from the Struldbruggs to the Yahoos is clear. The Yahoos are the culmination of the symbolic matrix Swift has created for the corruptions of man. They embody in a crude animal form most of the vices (and supposed glories) of civilized man. The most concretely disgusting of all the images Swift creates, they are also the most abstract symbol of man's irrational pursuit of power at the expense of reason. Swift makes clear in the last part of the fourth voyage that the Yahoos are not man himself any more than are the Houyhnhnms. But all the institutions of men are close to the fulfillment of a Yahoo nature

---

7. HD, xi, 196, 198 (TS, viii, 221, 223). Cf. Ernest Bernbaum's introduction to his edition of *Gulliver's Travels* (New York, Scribner's, 1920), p. xvii.

8. *Correspondence*, v, 246 (October 1735). The Struldbruggs "commonly acted like Mortals, till about Thirty Years old, after which by Degrees they grew melancholy and dejected, increasing in both till they came to Fourscore." HD, xi, 195-6 (TS, viii, 221).

as long as they remain in their inverted state. Created to embody rational control, to keep man decent like the brothers' coats, they are used instead to serve man's passions and desire for power over his fellows. It is this doubleness of all man's creations, and of man's nature itself, that Swift's irony constantly explores. He is, of course, exploiting a traditional classical view:

> A social instinct is implanted in all men by nature, and yet he who first founded the state was the greatest of benefactors. For man, when perfected, is the best of animals, but, when separated from law and justice, he is the worst of all; since armed injustice is the more dangerous, and he is equipped at birth with arms, meant to be used by intelligence and virtue, which he may use for the worst ends. Wherefore, if he have not virtue, he is most unholy and the most savage of animals, and the most full of lust and gluttony.[9]

But it is important to recall the full matrix into which Swift's symbols are placed for even a nominally Christian society. To men concerned with "our war with the world, the devil, and our own corrupt nature," the "most savage of animals" is not simply opposed to "the best of animals." When Swift prays he asks God to "make us hate every thing in ourselves that is unlike to thee." [1] The inversion is the greater for the greatness of the true end of man.

A COMPARISON OF METHODS

As we place the two works together, Swift's symbolic methods emerge more clearly, in their range and in their unity. Each of the works is recounted by an author who is the counterpart neither of Swift nor of the intelligent reader. Each author has his peculiar blindness, his own variant of the obliviousness which comes from excessive concentration on part of the truth. The two authors belong, however, to different rhetorical structures, and their characters are adapted to different satirical methods. The Tale Teller is garrulous and ingenious, full of explanations, proud of witty flights; Gulliver is spare in comment, literal minded, stolidly dedicated to factual reporting. The blindness of the Tale Teller emerges in a tissue of verbal contretemps; he is the victim of his own wit, which escapes his control and carries him along, a helpless rider, in a direction he does not intend. Gulliver's blindness becomes evident in his language

9. Aristotle, *Politics* (tr. Benjamin Jowett), Bk. I, chap. ii, 1253[a]. This passage has previously been cited by Theodore O. Wedel, "On the Philosophic Background of *Gulliver's Travels,*" *Studies in Philology, 23* (1926), 449–50. Cf. also Aristotle, *Politics,* Bk. VII, chap. xiii, 1332 [a, b], on the contrast between man and the animals.

1. *An Evening Prayer,* TS, III, 317, 315.

as the scenes he describes demand a moral judgment he has no capacity to make; but he is primarily the victim of events. The witty analogies which led to unexpected conclusions for the Tale Teller are embodied in the concrete world Gulliver inhabits; conclusions assert themselves as encounters with strange customs and strange peoples. Gulliver is trapped by circumstances, not words, and therefore cannot escape, as the Tale Teller does, an awareness of consequences. Gulliver does change in the last part of the book and to that extent at least comes closer to being a true fictional character than any of Swift's other ironic masks.

As the character of each author differs, so does the range of allusion which Swift can introduce. The very facility of the Tale Teller makes him the echo of a multitude of authors and serves to make the *Tale* itself a destructive parody of the solemn use of false wit. The manner of Gulliver is no less a parody but of a more limited kind: he reproduces the careful observation enjoined on mariners by the Royal Society.[2] Less extravagant and pretentious than the Tale Teller, he is less suggestive a figure, and his language contains less allusive parody. Yet the very simplicity of Gulliver allows him more readily to become a universal figure in a work whose rhetorical argument becomes increasingly general as it progresses.

Both the Tale Teller and Gulliver are versions of a typical Swiftian character—the fool who serves the knaves. The hypocrite is a more striking satirical subject in some ways, but he is too limited a figure, as superficial a representation of man as the Hobbesian image of thorough self-love or the sentimentalist's portrait of utter benevolence. The central issue for Swift is cognition. Whatever man's motives, selfish or not, a clear knowledge of his true interest will lead to virtue, and prudence will eventually become moral habit. This does not rule out a more transcendent virtue born directly of faith in God, obedience to His law, and imitation of divine virtues; but it does accept man at his worst and start from there, and it does make each man responsible for an error which common sense alone can avoid. The common dupe Swift invents, like his counterpart in the reader, is not clear sighted in selfishness; he is neither a rebel nor a Machiavel. A man of middling virtue, he would recoil from an accurate recognition of the ends he is promoting, and Swift, of course, never allows him that recognition but demands it instead of the reader. Rather, the fool among knaves is somewhat vain, somewhat proud, and very gullible. His shortsightedness can be exaggerated, as it is in much of Swift's satire, into a prepossession that ap-

2. See Ray W. Frantz, *The English Traveller and the Movement of Ideas 1660–1732, University Studies of the University of Nebraska, 32–3* (1932–33), 15–29 Especially valuable for Swift's parody of scientific style and thought are the two articles by Marjorie H. Nicolson and Nora V. Mohler, "The Scientific Background of Swift's Voyage to Laputa" and "Swift's 'Flying Island' in the Voyage to Laputa," *Annals of Science, 2* (1937), 299–334, 405–30.

proaches insanity. This kind of man is both too dense to be morally alert and too naïve to disguise his folly. Neither the Tale Teller nor Gulliver is the worst of his kind: each is a man seeking to defend more successful villains with a bathetic credulity. But as we can see in *A Modest Proposal,* the insanity of the fool becomes a metaphor for the guilt of responsible men.

The Tale Teller

The Tale Teller is not one of the "Wits of the present Age" like his "more successful Brethren the *Moderns.*" He is anxious to please, to be a "most devoted Servant of all *Modern* Forms," but he is somewhat uncomfortable among his younger contemporaries. Particularly does he resent the usurpation by Gresham and Will's—by the new scientists and wits—of the dignity of Grub Street. These are "revolted and new-fangled" offspring who deny the Grubean parents they have outdone.[3] The Tale Teller, then, is a modern *manqué,* aware of some limitations, free of some caprices, but only envious rather than critical of the brighter moderns. He is more tolerable than the knaves, less arrogant, more confused. He is old-fashioned enough to claim a rational pattern for, and to give the dignity of system to, the self-indulgence and competition of the moderns.

It is in the Epistle Dedicatory to Prince Posterity that we first encounter him, seeking to claim immortality for his brethren (having resigned it for himself). He cannot see Time's verdict as the impartial judgment of reason asserting itself inevitably over a long enough expanse but only as a "peculiar Malice" toward his own age. Unable to see, as the knaves are unwilling to admit, the age's own responsibility for this "universal Ruin," the Tale Teller projects his horror and fear into an extravagant image of Time as a cruel tyrant: "Be pleased to remark the Length and Strength, the Sharpness and Hardness, of his *Nails* and *Teeth:* Consider his baneful abominable *Breath,* Enemy to Life and Matter, infectious and corrupting."[4] But this very appeal to Posterity sets the Tale Teller off from his brethren, who scorn him as "a clown and pedant" for seeking works that have already been succeeded by fresher ones. As it turns out, he "can only avow in general . . . that we do abound in Learning and Wit; but to fix upon Particulars, is a Task too slippery for my slender Abilities."[5] The Tale Teller suffers from an excessive respect for fact; once the rational faculty is completely divorced from the empirical by the truer moderns, or by Peter and Jack, systems can be built more freely. The guise of the fool serves much the same function as the witty construction; it allows Swift to convert an argu-

3. HD, I, 24, 25, 27, 39 (TS, I, 39, 40, 42, 54).
4. HD, I, 19-20 (TS, I, 34-5).
5. HD, I, 21 (TS, I, 36).

ment into its opposite, just as he does by transforming Burnet's meta-phors.[6] In his treatment of Burnet, Swift in his own person is lightly defiant of logical strictness; here the Tale Teller is blunderingly industri-ous as he achieves the same end.

The Tale Teller is scarcely an admirable character at any point. As a representative of a "Corporation of Poets," he is devoted to the forms of his "refined Age." For all his difficulties he is frightfully vain, both as "author of this miraculous treatise" and as the heir of man's inevita-ble progress. Having spent his years writing "Four-score and eleven Pamphlets . . . for the Service of six and thirty Factions," he can look back with "unspeakable Comfort" at having "passed a long Life, with a Conscience void of Offence." Yet his venality has an irresponsible innocence about it; he still offers himself as "Secretary" of the universe, willing to elucidate all mysteries for "the general Good of Mankind." [7] In his eagerness to defend the indefensible he becomes a throwback to another kind of devout wit. Since the slightness of modern works can be denied only if we consider these works the vehicles of hidden truths, the Tale Teller becomes much like the Christian virtuoso of the seven-teenth century who reads signs of God's wisdom in the meanest of natu-ral phenomena. It is the attitude we find constantly in Sir Thomas Browne or in Robert Boyle's *Occasional Reflections,* which Swift parodied in the *Meditation upon a Broomstick.* Lady Berkeley remarked, when Swift announced the title of the pretended meditation of Boyle, "What a strange subject! But there is no knowing what useful lessons of instruction this wonderful man may draw from things apparently the most trivial." [8] This ingenuity has in the moderns the inverted motive of revealing the greater glory not of God but of themselves.

Appropriately, Swift recalls the equation common in the century be-hind him, of the extravagant doctrines of dissenters and such heresies as those of the Gnostics.[9] Both split Christianity with schism, both are justified by the wresting of Scripture, both are instruments of pride and dominion. In placing on his title page an epigraph from Irenaeus quoting the jargon of the Gnostics, Swift allies himself with the church fathers and identifies the moderns with the speculative heretics. Even more, Swift adds a passage from Lucretius wherein new flowers, un-like any previously offered, are sought. The moderns can only turn to the variety of disease if they repudiate the health of the ancients as trite or commonplace. The Tale Teller, like the Gnostics, attempts great sub-tlety. In this he is akin to all possessed fools who would prove the truth

6. See above, chap. iii, pp. 49–50.
7. HD, I, 42, 77 (TS, I, 57, 89).
8. TS, I, 332. Cf. Swift's remark: "Boyle was a very silly writer." *Remarks on Bur-net's History of His Own Times,* TS, x, 338.
9. See above, chap. i, p. 6.

of their fancies. All of them wrest Scripture in one way or another—
the virtuoso forcing the evidence of nature, Bentley quarrying literary
texts for historical evidence, Thomas Vaughan ceaselessly and fantasti-
cally referring "all naturals to their spirituals by the way of secret analogy." [1]

In Vaughan and the dark authors Swift found the most direct heirs
of the Gnostics and also the most conspicuously nonsensical theorizers
of speculative fancies. Vaughan, in words reminiscent of Donne, urged
a departure from too narrow a reading of Scripture:

> That which I now write must needs appear very strange and incredi-
> ble to the common man, whose knowledge sticks in the bark of al-
> legories and mystical speeches, never apprehending that which is signi-
> fied by them unto us. This, I say, must needs sound strange with such
> as understand the Scriptures in the literal, plain sense, considering not
> the scope and intention of the Divine Spirit, by whom they were first
> penned and delivered. [2]

Not only did Vaughan profess to reveal the mysteries in Scripture but
he turned as well, for his magical doctrine, to oral tradition, as does
Peter in the *Tale*. Some things, Vaughan explained, "which exceeded
carnal understanding were transmitted without writing." [3] Centuries
before, Irenaeus had complained of the Gnostics that "they disregard the
order and connection of the Scriptures," that they "patch together old
wives' fables, and then endeavour, by violently drawing [words] away
from their proper connection . . . to adapt the oracles of God to their
baseless fictions." They "desert what is certain, indubitable, and true"
and, like the sophists interpreting Homer, collect scattered expressions
and "twist them" to their own sense. [4] Swift might have looked back
beyond Irenaeus to Plato, whose attack upon rhapsode and sophist resembles Swift's treatment of inverted wit. As the sophists claimed to
extract all kinds of wisdom from Homer, Swift's moderns seem to imply
the presence of such wisdom in their own writings. It is only appropriate, therefore, that the moderns should scorn Homer for his inadequacy
in providing a "compleat Body of all Knowledge Human, Divine, Politi-

1. Thomas Vaughan, *Anima Magica Abscondita,* in *Works,* ed. Arthur E. Waite
(London, Theosophical Publishing House, 1919), p. 116. The fullest account of the
immediate background of the *Tale* and of Swift's use of it for satire and parody is
in Starkman, *Swift's Satire on Learning in A Tale of a Tub.* There is a valuable discussion of Swift's use of Thomas Vaughan in pp. 45–56.
2. Vaughan, *Anthroposophia Theomagica,* in *Works,* ed. Waite, p. 36.
3. *Ibid.,* p. 37.
4. Irenaeus, *Against Heresies,* Bk. I, chaps. viii, ix; Bk. II, chap. xxvii, in *The Ante
Nicene Fathers,* ed. Alexander Roberts, James Donaldson, and A. C. Coxe (Buffalo
1885), I, 326, 330, 399.

cal, and Mechanick," for his imperfect knowledge of Jacob Boehme, and for his unreliable cure for syphilis.[5]

In the spirit of modern subtlety the Tale Teller urges greater penetration (that is, credulity) upon his readers:

> But the greatest Maim given to that general Reception, which the Writings of our Society have formerly received, (next to the transitory State of all sublunary Things), hath been a superficial Vein among many Readers of the present Age, who will by no means be persuaded to inspect beyond the Surface and the Rind of Things; whereas, *Wisdom* is a *Fox,* who after long hunting, will at last cost you the Pains to dig out: 'Tis a *Cheese,* which by how much the richer, has the thicker, the homelier, and the courser Coat; and whereof to a judicious Palate, the *Maggots* are the best. 'Tis a *Sack-Posset,* wherein the deeper you go, you will find it the sweeter. *Wisdom* is a *Hen,* whose *Cackling* we must value and consider, because it is attended with an *Egg;* But then, lastly, 'tis a *Nut,* which, unless you chuse with Judgment, may cost you a Tooth, and pay you with nothing but a *Worm.*[6]

Here we can see all the devices at work. The figure of the rind and the kernel was a commonplace popular throughout the seventeenth century and long before. The Tale Teller argues from analogy, with vivacity and copiousness of wit, but his analogies gradually become less and less apt. From a praise of the reward which costs pains he turns to a praise of pains which yield a reward. The instance of the maggots throws doubt on the value of the reward, and the instance of the hen uses the reward not only to justify the means but to dignify all accompanying annoyances. Finally Swift turns to new effect a sentence he probably found in Dryden. Dryden wrote of Cleveland that "he gives us many times a hard nut to break our teeth without a kernel for our pains." [7] It is Swift's peculiar genius to make of Dryden's sharp figure an even sharper one; he gives more than an image of futile pains, he creates revulsion as well. It is not merely folly which Swift is castigating but a perversion of values.

It is the special gift of the Tale Teller to be able to reach a damaging conclusion with no discomposure and move on with only a complacent reference to "these momentous Truths." We can see the same composed self-exposure in his encouragement to satirists: "but let them remember, it is with *Wits* as with *Razors,* which are never so apt to *cut* those they are employ'd on, as when they have *lost their Edge.* Besides, those whose

5. HD, I, 79–80 (TS, I, 91–2).

6. HD, I, 40 (TS, I, 54–5). This passage and the next have also been discussed by Robert C. Elliott, "Swift's *Tale of a Tub:* An Essay in Problems of Structure," *PMLA,* 66 (1951), 448–9, 453. The whole article (pp. 441–55) is relevant to this chapter.

7. John Dryden, *An Essay of Dramatic Poesy,* in *Essays,* ed. W. P. Ker (Oxford, Clarendon Press, 1926), I, 52.

Teeth are too rotten to bite, are best of all others, qualified to revenge that Defect with their Breath." [8] The function of razors casually shifts from shaving to cutting; it can then be blandly assumed that teeth are meant only for wounding. Again the reversal of true values is made disgusting as well as foolish: if destruction is the real purpose, the foulest means are available to the least competent.

One can find many such ironic reversals in *A Tale of a Tub,* woven together into a web of imperturbable sweet reasonableness:

> The *True Criticks* are known by their Talent of swarming about the noblest Writers, to which they are carried meerly by Instinct, as a Rat to the best Cheese, or a Wasp to the fairest Fruit. So, when the *King* is a Horse-back, he is sure to be the *dirtiest* Person of the Company, and they that make their Court best, are such as *bespatter* him most.

Nor does the author rest with these analogies; he has still another to make complete the reversal of standards:

> Lastly; A *True Critick,* in the Perusal of a Book, is like a *Dog* at a Feast, whose Thoughts and Stomach are wholly set upon what the Guests *fling away,* and consequently, is apt to *Snarl* most, when there are fewest *Bones.*

This is the kind of passage which illustrates the richness of Swift's wit. The Tale Teller has no purpose but to show his talent for creating figures. But all the terms allow extension. The "feast" provides us with the suggestion not only of true nourishment (as opposed to the corrupt diet of the moderns) and pleasure but also of the decorum of hospitality. This decorum is a constant theme in Swift; we see it in the grace of the bee's flight or the decency of the brothers' original coats, just as we see the counterpart of the snarling dog in the angry spider or the rudeness of the foppish Peter. The eye for faults becomes an appetite for them, just as the raking together of the dung of Augeas' stables becomes an end in itself, and both reversals recall the worm in the nut. What other ages, the true guests, have neglected and flung away as worthless is the only diet the moderns will allow themselves. The Tale Teller's wit lacks order or purpose of its own, but it serves Swift's own rhetorical ends at every point. [9]

A few conclusions about Swift's attitudes may be drawn from his practice in *A Tale of a Tub.* False wit can lead us wherever we want to go; reasoning by analogy can, in the hands of a fool or a sophister,

8. HD, I, 29–30 (TS, I, 45).
9. HD, I, 63–4 (TS, I, 78). Cf. also HD, I, 58 (TS, I, 72): "from this Heavenly Descent of *Criticism,* and the close Analogy it bears to *Heroick Virtue,* 'tis easie to Assign the proper Employment of a *True Ancient Genuine Critick;* which is, to travel thro' this vast World of Writings; to pursue and hunt those Monstrous Faults bred within them: to drag out the lurking Errors like *Cacus* from his Den; to multiply them like *Hydra's* Heads; and rake them together like *Augeas's* Dung."

be used to reach any conclusion. Speculative interpretation which thrives upon such false wit can maintain constant warfare within religion. Each zealot may battle for his own interest under the banners of whatever sanctions he can wrest from Scripture. Thus the departure from common forms and common sense makes hypocrisy possible for the conscious knaves and gives them countless gullible dupes. The same is true in the realm of politics: we can see in the *Examiner* or in the replies to Burnet and the Irish dissenters Swift's resistance to that manipulation of words which makes them a cloak for one's own ambition. One must constantly place these words in new contexts, test their application, purge them of false power. Otherwise each man becomes his own Partridge or Bickerstaff, finding what he will in the influence of the stars, winning credulity without responsibility of proof but with all the authority of supernatural wisdom. This is the implicit critique of false wit. Recognized for what it is, however, it can become a brilliant satirical device.

The most important function of the Tale Teller in the structure of the work is his gradual absorption of a vast range of folly in his panegyric and imitation. The power of the *Tale* arises not so much from a tight and economical structure as from the unpredictable extension that is given a few commanding principles. Its unity is one of "repetitive form," the "consistent maintaining of a principle under new guises." [1] Its economy comes of the deftness with which Swift makes the same symbolic pattern work again and again, each time including a new victim, who in turn represents a new field of achievement. The pattern itself is intensified more and more, from folly to bestiality, from bestiality to mechanism.

The point at which the meanings of the *Tale* become most general and inclusive is the "Digression concerning the Original, the Use and Improvement of Madness in a Commonwealth." Madness becomes the common term for all the abuses of reason and sources of greatness in the *Tale,* much as the Yahoos provide the basic pattern of civilized society in *Gulliver's Travels.* Where Gulliver is sufficiently human to be disgusted by the Yahoos, the Tale Teller glorifies madness, only regretting the waste of powers which the confinement of Bedlam represents. It is as if Gulliver were to bring home a Yahoo to be prime minister. In defending madness the Tale Teller looks upon reason with the same irrational horror he earlier showed toward Time:

> then comes Reason officiously, with Tools for cutting, and opening, and mangling, and piercing, offering to demonstrate that they [bodies] are not of the same consistence quite thro'. Now, I take all this to be the last Degree of perverting Nature; one of whose Eternal Laws it is, to put her best Furniture forward. [2]

1. Kenneth Burke, *Counter-Statement* (New York, Harcourt, Brace, 1931), p. 159.
2. HD, I, 109 (TS, I, 120).

This last phrase recalls the clothes worshippers' account of God as a tailor and *"Journey-man* Nature" as a valet to the *"vegetable* Beaux." [3] In what follows one finds the same distortion of imagination :

> And therefore, in order to save the Charges of all such expensive Anatomy for the Time to come; I do here think fit to inform the Reader, that in such Conclusions as these, Reason is certainly in the Right; and that in most Corporeal Beings, which have fallen under my Cognizance, the *Outside* has been infinitely preferable to the *In:* Whereof I have been farther convinced from some late Experiments. Last Week I saw a Woman flay'd, and you will hardly believe, how much it altered her Person for the worse.

The last sentence becomes significant only through being the calm assertion of a man without normal awareness. The Tale Teller is able to equate reason with cutting, analysis with flaying, just as he has easily turned the pursuit of wisdom into the enjoyment of obscurity. All the inversions we have seen before are brought to focus here. The rind has replaced the kernel and clothes the man. The digression has overwhelmed the tale. Fancy is astride reason. The body governs the soul. Most generally, the outside has replaced the inside. So the Tale Teller can argue for contentment with "the *Films* and *Images* that fly off upon his senses from the *Superficies* of Things" and placidly expose his own argument with a conclusion that negates all his praise :

> Such a Man truly wise, creams off Nature, leaving the Sower and the Dregs for Philosophy and Reason to lap up. This is the sublime and refined Point of Felicity, called *the Possession of being well deceived;* The Serene Peaceful State of being a Fool among Knaves. [4]

The Tale Teller has reduced the choice to carping or serenity, and from this opposition the true nature of reason has escaped. We need hardly assume that Swift accepts either alternative for himself or that he means the reader to be completely frustrated. Man is neither the beau's suit nor his dissected body. True poetry is neither the modern effusion nor the ancient fragments Bentley has collected. Proper food is neither a ragout nor the bones flung under the table, proper dress neither gold fringe nor rags, and the true church, for Swift, is neither Peter's nor Jack's. The middle way demands a harmony of outside and inside, a decent coat which always fits. To choose between inside and outside is either to seek a transcendent purity impossible for man or to settle for mere appearance to the neglect of spirit. It is by some such principle as this that Swift's symbols work in *A Tale of a Tub.* The structure of the book, by a series of ironic reversals, reduces the Tale Teller's praise

3. HD, I, 47 (TS, I, 61).
4. HD, I, 110 (TS, I, 120–1).

of his fellows to the exposure of a few principles of physiological compulsion. But if the drives are few, simple, and low, there is complexity enough. It lies not in the riches of wit that the Tale Teller claims but in the unfailing ingenuity of rationalization, the enormous effort exerted to escape from seeing oneself as one is and from submitting to the discipline of becoming better. The style of the Tale Teller is itself a symbol of this complexity which is really simplicity, a distortion of meanings that is no better than an incapacity for them: "it is the Nature of Rags to bear a kind of mock Resemblance to Finery; there being a sort of fluttering Appearance in both, which is not to be distinguished at a Distance, in the Dark, or by short-sighted Eyes." [5]

Lemuel Gulliver

For Lemuel Gulliver, the tradition of travel books provided Swift with a useful type, the voyager whose judgment is easily corrupted either by his pleasure in the strange or by his complacent condescension toward it. He may be the innovator finding new models or the proud patriot defying any challenge to his own or to his countrymen's superiority. In either case, a faithful report of his responses arouses sentiments in the detached reader quite different from his own. Gulliver's meticulously accurate report of the Lilliputians is altogether surface observation and produces the kind of understatement that neglects completely the overtones of an experience. This is heightened by Gulliver's casual insertion of a human scale at those moments when increments of size are the mark of Lilliputian grandeur. The emperor, Gulliver tells us, "is taller by almost the Breadth of my Nail, than any of his Court; which alone is enough to strike an Awe into the Beholders." [6] Just as he is oblivious to these overtones of pettiness, so Gulliver can take Lilliputian dignities at their face value, especially when they are conferred on him. Suspected of adultery with Flimnap's wife, he does not recognize the incongruity of the charge. He is simply concerned with the lady's reputation and his own: "I had the Honour to be a *Nardac,* which the Treasurer himself is not; for all the World knows he is only a *Clumglum,* a title inferior by one Degree, as that of a Marquess is to a Duke in *England;* yet I allow he preceded me in right of his Post." Even when Gulliver has been completely betrayed and considers destroying the Lilliputians, he is restrained in part by his gratitude to the little emperor for "the high Title of *Nardac* he conferred upon me." [7]

5. HD, I, 128 (TS, I, 137).
6. HD, XI, 14 (TS, VIII, 29).
7. HD, XI, 50, 57 (TS, VIII, 67, 74). Pride is a consistent theme in the four voyages. In Laputa, Gulliver's chief grievance is not the falseness of the learning but the fact that he is scorned for not being adept in it. HD, XI, 157 (TS, VIII, 180). In Brobdingnag, at first fearing death under the tread of the giants, Gulliver comes to resent that the

To an extent Gulliver has the virtues of the Drapier in being a man whose understanding cannot go beyond certain limits. When the setting becomes most transparently an English one, for example, Gulliver's humble station is also invoked. In his conversations with the Houyhnhnm he shows considerable acquaintance with royal courts, but in Lilliput he is still unable to penetrate the refinements of ministers' cabals. When he learns that his eyes are to be put out and that he is to be starved to death he confesses that "having never been designed for a Courtier either by my Birth or Education, I was so ill a Judge of Things, that I could not discover the *Lenity* and Favour of this Sentence; but conceived it (perhaps erroneously) rather to be rigorous than gentle." [8] The Lilliputians themselves are beyond difficulties of this sort. Although nothing terrifies them "so much as those Encomiums on his Majesty's Mercy," the simple reversal of meaning in court decrees is, like the constant disputes over trivial symbols, part of the logic by which they live. They are untroubled by need for rationalization of such absurdities. Gulliver is troubled but not, like the Drapier, defiant. He is too deferential toward authority to insist upon common sense.

Since the satiric distortions are postulated as the real world and Gulliver's insensibility leaves him unaware of their significance, Swift can direct special attention throughout the book to the drama of incomprehension and the problem of meaning. Gulliver's insensibility is increased, if not actually caused, by his satisfaction with man's rational powers and all they have achieved. The mind which accepts Lilliput without contempt becomes in Brobdingnag a mind which takes childish pride in feats remarkable only in that one so diminutive can perform them. Many of the feats end in disaster: the stunned linnet comes to life, Gulliver's leap does not quite clear the dung. These disasters set the pattern of the conversation with the Brobdingnagian king. There Gulliver's pride is extended to European man, whose achievements are Gulliver's own claim to importance and to rational powers. What follows is comparable to the Tale Teller's appeal to Prince Posterity. In this case the detachment of distance replaces the hostility of Time. The king makes notes as Gulliver testifies in behalf of mankind, and the panegyric supplies the evidence for an indictment. All that Gulliver neglects is what he has seen in Lilliput, the difference between the original institutions and the corrupt practices of men. The king concludes: "My little Friend *Grildrig;*

Maids of Honor treat him "without any Manner of Ceremony, like a Creature who had no Sort of Consequence." HD, XI, 103 (TS, VIII, 121). Cf. Swift's ironic remarks in a letter to Mrs. Howard (27 November 1726): "I am not such a prostitute flatterer as Gulliver, whose chief study is to extenuate the vices, and magnify the virtues, of mankind, and perpetually dins our ears with the praises of his country in the midst of corruption, and for that reason alone has found so many readers, and probably will have a pension, which, I suppose, was his chief design in writing." *Correspondence,* III, 366.

8. HD, XI, 56 (TS, VIII, 74).

you have made a most admirable Panegyrick upon your country. You have clearly proved that Ignorance, Idleness, and Vice, are the proper Ingredients for qualifying a Legislator. That Laws are best explained, interpreted, and applied by those whose Interest and Abilities lie in perverting, confounding, and eluding them." [9] Gulliver's pride serves even more effectively than the Tale Teller's ingenuity to damn his fellows. In the manner of the Tale Teller he can shrug off "so remote a Prince's Notions of Virtue and Vice" and console himself with the superiority of the "politer Countries of *Europe*." But the achievements of which he can boast are not merely trivial or ridiculous; the range and intensity of the satire have greatly increased. Gulliver offers the king the means of becoming "absolute Master of the Lives, the Liberties, and the Fortunes of his People." [1] This is a rejection of all the scruples which prevented Gulliver from completing the conquest of Blefuscu, but the inconsistency is partially explained by Gulliver's experience at Lilliput. Having learned there the nature of kings and courts, he seeks to win this king's favor by appealing to his desire for power. He is awed by the learning which has "reduced *Politicks* into a *Science*," and he is unable to see its moral significance. Conversely, Gulliver can dismiss as "visionary" those few political projectors in Lagado who have a rational program. [2]

Gulliver's change in the fourth voyage is largely an emotional conversion. Having resisted all the lessons which have confronted him in the first three voyages, he is now led into a dilemma. Although he expects to meet "Savages," he fails to recognize the Yahoos as more than intensely disagreeable animals. His antipathy is aroused before his pride can operate: he unknowingly sees the human animal for the first time without the adornment of dress or civilization. It is only when the Houyhnhnms arrange a juxtaposition that Gulliver sees with horror "in this abominable Animal, a perfect human Figure." His pride in man comes too late: "although there were few greater Lovers of Mankind, at that time, than myself; yet I confess I never saw any sensitive Being so detestable on all Accounts." [3] Gulliver can only hope to save himself from identification with the Yahoos, and his clothes become his sole defense.

Once the secret of the clothes is revealed and Gulliver's physical identity with the Yahoos is established, he seeks to establish himself as at least a rational Yahoo. Gulliver still smarts at the application of that term to himself, but the lack of any other term in the Houyhnhnm language enforces its use. The limited experience which Swift postulates for the Houyhnhnms serves, therefore, to make the dilemma inescapable. The

9. HD, XI, 116 (TS, VIII, 135).
1. HD, XI, 117, 119 (TS, VIII, 138, 139).
2. HD, XI, 171 (TS, VIII, 195).
3. HD, XI, 207, 214 (TS, VIII, 231, 238–9).

dilemma is as false as that created by the Tale Teller in the digression on madness. In both cases the extremes are presented as necessary alternatives, and the mean is ignored. In this case, the false dilemma is created largely by Gulliver's pride, turning from deluded complacency only to deluded misanthropy. Allowed only the name of Yahoo, Gulliver must prove mankind rational in order to escape the stigma of complete identification with the brutes. His account of man founders almost at once; in describing his crew, he reveals a full catalogue of human vice:

> Some were undone by Law-suits; others spent all they had in Drinking, Whoring and Gaming; others fled for Treason; many for Murder, Theft, Poysoning, Robbery, Perjury, Forgery, Coining false Money; for committing Rapes or Sodomy; for flying from their Colours, or deserting to the Enemy; and most of them had broken Prison. None of these durst return to their native Countries for fear of being hanged, or of starving in a Jail; and therefore were under the Necessity of seeking a Livelihood in other Places.[4]

Gulliver's description of Europe is one of the triumphs of the book. We are prepared for Gulliver's new antipathy to his own kind by his reference to "our barbarous *English*" language.[5] It becomes clear by the time he has finished that he is no longer interested in saving appearances. He has given up the defense of fellow men and hopes only to be able to cast his lot with the Houyhnhnms. His pride can be saved only by winning their favor. Gulliver's account is limited, moreover, by the language in which he must speak, by the remoteness of the Houyhnhnms from all human conceptions, and by his strict adherence to truth. What follows is a picture of human institutions simplified in much the manner of the mythical Lilliput and Laputa. In this section, however, Gulliver is describing a literal Europe.

In missing the moral significance of what he has previously described, Gulliver has also missed its symbolic import; he sees the Lilliputians as a strange people but not as a representation of man's pettiness. Throughout his travels Gulliver is incapable of perceiving relationships, and Swift has deliberately placed him in a world of semiallegorical relationships. He has remained indifferent to all but appearances, never venturing to see the appearances as significant of anything but themselves. His account of Europe has the same simplification Gulliver has learned to accept without question in the symbolic world of his travels. Accustomed to moving among symbols (really, among aspects of man) as if they were solid realities, he has little difficulty in reducing reality to the same symbolic patterns.[6] His typical understatement, in these new circum-

4. HD, XI, 228 (TS, VIII, 252).
5. HD, XI, 229 (TS, VIII, 253).
6. See Horrell, "What Gulliver Knew," *Sewanee Review*, pp. 482–4.

stances, becomes overstatement. All that he has seen finds its counterpart in the picture of Europe—the inversion of institutions and of the meanings of words, the limitless appetites without avowal or control, the ingenuities of intellect turned to display or rationalization, and the juxtaposition of dignity and decay, of pride and filth. But his picture presents only the comic surface of epicyclic complication, of constant reversal, and of inhuman mechanism. It is a picture which assembles all the degraded gestures with no attempt to explain their purpose or their cause. Thus Gulliver can tell the Houyhnhnm that "a *Soldier* is a *Yahoo* hired to kill in cold Blood as many of his own Species, who have never offended him, as possibly he can." This divorces the soldier from patriotism or duty and the means of killing from the end; one need not commend war to recognize it as something more than this. In places this method of distortion becomes comparable to the Lilliputian travesty or to the allegorical events of the *Tale:*

> Difference in Opinions hath cost many Millions of Lives: For Instance, whether *Flesh* be *Bread,* or *Bread* be *Flesh:* Whether the Juice of a certain *Berry* be *Blood* or *Wine:* Whether *Whistling* be a Vice or a Virtue: Whether it be better to *kiss* a Post, or throw it into the Fire: What is the best Colour for a *Coat,* whether, *Black, White, Red,* or *Grey;* and whether it should be *long* or *short, narrow* or *wide, dirty* or *clean;* with many more.[7]

Once Gulliver has presented the picture of human society drained of all nobility and even of purpose, the Houyhnhnm master can draw the relationship for him. By setting aside some of the achievements of man in "Learning, Government, Arts, Manufactures, and the like," and by amplifying the qualities of the Yahoos, the Houyhnhnm finds a "Parity" in their natures. "He went through all our Vices and Follies, and discovered many which I had never mentioned to him; by only supposing what Qualities a *Yahoo* of their Country, with a small Proportion of Reason, might be capable of exerting: And concluded, with too much Probability, how vile as well as miserable such a Creature must be." [8] It is the simplest of relationships, the identity of man and Yahoo. The Houyhnhnm, who is unacquainted with the possibility of rational creatures other than of his own kind, is reluctant to admit a new species as long as man can be accounted for in terms of previous experience. He has no animus, therefore, in drawing the damning equation; his conclusion is the result of cool logic. Once Gulliver has come to accept this identity, he has reached the limits of his comprehension. He has no conception of a relationship that is less than identity. He can no more distinguish the corrupt Yahoo pattern from man's total behavior than he

7. HD, xi, 230–1 (TS, viii, 254–5).
8. HD, xi, 246, 262 (TS, viii, 273, 289).

can abstract the rational pattern of the Houyhnhnms' life from their passionless embodiment of it. He has arrived at no generalizations, no lessons: he can only hope to resemble a Houyhnhnm so that he will not be taken for a Yahoo. We have seen the Tale Teller saving the world of appearance by drawing relationships which comfort his pride but distort the nature of reality. Gulliver is no less a victim of appearance in his failure to draw relationships. Thoroughly empirical, he can follow models but cannot grasp principles. Thoroughly literal, he can respond to images but not to their metaphorical significance. His world is a world of outsides, not by choice as for the Tale Teller but by necessity. Having believed that man is a rational animal, now finally convinced of his error, his solution is to worship the only thoroughly rational animal he has encountered.

The close of the book shows Gulliver suffering from a kind of inverted pride, a hatred of all humankind for the qualities which he himself shares. The encounter with Pedro de Mendez illustrates this very well; he is, according to Gulliver, a "very courteous and generous Person," but only with reluctance does Gulliver *descend* "to treat him like an Animal which had some little Portion of Reason." [9] The final absurdity is Gulliver's affection for his horses' conversation and his intolerance of the smell and presence of his own family. As he has returned from Brobdingnag with a visual maladjustment but no moral improvement, so now he has acquired the convert's zeal for Houyhnhnm mannerisms (even to a whinnying voice and an equine gait) but with no real sense of their meaning. Yet Gulliver's madness and projector's enthusiasm do not altogether undercut his charge. This madness, in a wiser man, would be the *splendida bilis* of the satirist, the only sanity in a perverted world. One need not accept Gulliver's picture of man, but one cannot neglect the partial truth which it reveals. It is not the human animal as such he attacks in his saner moments but the animal's engrossment of the tribute due to virtue, reason, and nature:

> My Reconcilement to the *Yahoo*-kind in general might not be so difficult, if they would be content with those Vices and Follies only which Nature hath entitled them to. I am not in the least provoked at the Sight of a Lawyer, a Pickpocket, a Colonel, a Fool, a Lord, a Gamester, a Politician, a Whoremonger, a Physician, an Evidence, a Suborner, an Attorney, a Traytor, or the like. This is all according to the due Course of Things: But, when I behold a Lump of Deformity, and Diseases both in Body and Mind, smitten with Pride, it immediately breaks all the Measures of my Patience; neither shall I be ever able to comprehend how such an Animal and such a Vice could tally together.[1]

9. HD, xi, 271 (TS, viii, 298).
1. HD, xi, 280 (TS, viii, 307).

The use of "Nature" in this passage is ironic enough, but it suggests a middle view that Gulliver hardly perceives. Both the Houyhnhnms and the Yahoos live according to a nature simpler than man's—the Houyhnhnms with a rationality which no passions or appetites disturb, the Yahoos with appetites their cunning can only serve. Both are free of responsibility: the Houyhnhnm's intuition is never clouded by error, the Yahoo's grossness is disgusting but incorrigible. The responsibility of man is imposed by the presence both of conflict and of capacity for change. His moral duties are the counterpart of his industry in the world:

> The motions of the sun and moon, in short, the whole system of the universe . . . are in the utmost degree of regularity and perfection; but wherever God hath left to man the power of interposing a remedy by thought or labour, there he hath placed things in a state of imperfection, on purpose to stir up human industry, without which life would stagnate, or indeed rather could not subsist at all.[2]

Pride, of all vices, most robs man of the clear self-knowledge which awakens his sense of responsibility, and it is appropriate that Gulliver attack it. But it is notable that even as he attacks it Gulliver is its victim. The irony is sustained to the last. Gulliver, who began with a pride in man that found him above criticism, ends with a pride in pure reason that finds man insupportable. Even as he warns men of the vice of pride, he entreats "those who have any Tincture of this absurd Vice, that they will not presume to appear in my Sight." Gulliver plans, he tells us, "to behold my Figure often in a Glass, and thus if possible to habituate my self by Time to tolerate the Sight of a human Creature." [3] The obvious injunction is one that Auden has framed in a similar case of illusion and resultant despair:

> O look, look in the mirror,
>   O look in your distress;
> Life remains a blessing
>   Although you cannot bless.
>
> O stand, stand at the window
>   As the tears scald and start;
> You shall love your crooked neighbor
>   With your crooked heart.[4]

Throughout the four voyages a rhetorical pattern is prepared by linkages between apparently discrete events. Gulliver does not connect these events and so cannot learn from experience, but the pattern is evident to the reader. The "utopian" sections, for example, are clearly an embodi-

2. *Thoughts on Various Subjects*, TS, I, 279.
3. HD, XI, 280, 279 (TS, VIII, 308, 306).
4. W. H. Auden, "As I Walked Out One Evening," *Collected Poetry* (New York, Random House, 1945), p. 198.

ment of reason but not necessarily the only possible embodiment or that best suited to the human animal. They serve as a standard of rational behavior if not as a model for human practice. This rational pattern, a neglected possibility in Lilliput, is repeated again and again —with modifications in Brobdingnag, by suggestion in the estate of Lord Munodi and the historical visions of Glubbdubdrib, explicitly in the life of the Houyhnhnms.[5] We are prepared to see rationality in a static, simple society and to associate motion and force with irrational programs of conquest. The physical horror of the body is introduced, without much awareness, by Gulliver in the first voyage; it becomes his preoccupation in Brobdingnag and is constantly evoked throughout the third voyage. We are prepared for the wedding of irrational conquest with physical grossness in the filthy and competitive Yahoos. There is, then, in *Gulliver's Travels* a weaving together of motifs not unlike that of *A Tale of a Tub*. In the *Tale* we are constantly shocked by new linkages blandly discovered by the ingenious Tale Teller. In the *Travels* the linkages remain implicit. A matrix is prepared unobtrusively instead of explicitly; its full range is revealed not gradually but suddenly, and its revelation affects Gulliver profoundly, as the Tale Teller is never affected. The difference in method can be likened to the differences we have seen on the level of style. *A Tale of a Tub* is close to the false wit of the poems. The witty transformations are made openly; the surprise comes largely from unpredictable extravagance being turned to aptness. *Gulliver's Travels* resembles the works in the plain style which seem to be doing one thing while they accomplish another, whose apparent flatness is designed to distract us from their rhetorical complexity. Both works are ironical, but the irony is much more in command of *Gulliver's Travels* than of the *Tale;* it is not sacrificed to local effects of wit, and it has acquired dramatic force. *A Tale of a Tub* is a more inventive work and perhaps richer in suggestion, but it lacks the rhetorical precision which steadily prepares the enormous weight of meaning that is carried in the final symbols of *Gulliver's Travels*.

5. There has been a tendency in recent critics to find the Houyhnhnms inherently ludicrous. Swift's rational horses are clearly no model for man, and it seems as much beside the point to deny the appeal of their life as to follow Gulliver in succumbing to it. The Houyhnhnms are, of course, entirely "natural": they are unaware of "things . . . above our reason" such as Swift treats in his sermon *On the Trinity*. Their life is, like that of animals guided by "unerring" instinct, both more orderly and less complex than that of man. See Pope, *An Essay on Man*, ed. Mack, Epistle III, line 83, and note to lines 83–98, p. 100. It is important to see Gulliver's folly in taking the Houyhnhnms as a model for man, but there is a danger of multiplying ironies. If we consider the Houyhnhnm life ludicrous in itself, we are likely to fall into the Mandevillian celebration of a corrupt world for its richness and complexity. Most versions of heaven show it as simpler than the world, and Shaw's Satan, for one, makes much of that disagreeable fact. The pattern of *Gulliver's Travels* as a whole makes the Houyhnhnms the culmination of the rationality suggested in the three earlier voyages. In revealing the "inside," Swift has divested it entirely; we can look back to the mediation of "inside" and "outside" of Brobdingnag as a possible model. See below, pp. 105–6.

VI

Patterns of Meaning: A Summary

SWIFT is distrustful of heroism but not altogether skeptical. Throughout his work we find warnings that the deliverer we introduce may turn out to be a worse oppressor than those he destroys. Yet he can speak of Stella's courage with obvious reverence, and muted as it is, there is a heroic ideal implied throughout his works. It is a heroism of moderation. First of all, courage must be divorced from "our endless *Itch* of Pow'r." [1] The true heroes are men out of power, like Lord Munodi, or martyrs and near martyrs, like Thomas More in the past or Harley in the present (the Harley whose policy was too moderate for all extreme factions, who was almost stabbed to death while in office and brought to trial when he was out). To this list one might add the retired Temple, the nonjuring Sancroft, the anonymous Athenian Society of the early odes, and of course Swift himself and his friends in the Hanoverian era. [2] When the heroic role is played by a man in power, like the king of Brobdingnag, he is a man unwilling to extend his power or indeed to use it for private ends. Second, the heroes of moderation are singular only in their resistance to tyranny, whether of a man or a fashion. They have the rare integrity which dissociates good sense from the will of the majority; they find truth in the balance of interests rather than in the predominant interest. They are eager to stem corruption or to remove it, but they have no sanguine hope of achieving original purity; their ends are practical—the possible solution rather than the overambitious goal which can never be attained. Swift himself in the *Advancement of Religion* makes a proposal that may seem cynical to those who expect too much of man; he would have the queen propagate virtue by making it profitable, in the hope that what is done for profit may ultimately become habitual. [3] One might say that the heroes of moderation

1. The phrase occurs in "A Panegyric on Dean Swift," *Poems*, II, 493, line 10.
2. See, e.g., *Letters to Ford*, p. 171 (Ford's letter to Swift, 8 July 1736) ; *Correspondence*, V, 427 (Pope to Swift, 23 March 1736/7) ; *Correspondence*, V, 143 (Swift to Pulteney, 8 March 1734/5).
3. *A Project for the Advancement of Religion, and the Reformation of Manners*, HD, II, 59 (TS, III, 43) : "our Duty, by becoming our Interest, would take Root in our Natures, and mix with the very Genius of our People." Cf. the sermon *On the Poor Man's Contentment*: "But this is indeed one Part of your Happiness, that the Lowness of your Condition, in a Manner, forceth you to what is pleasing to God, and necessary for your daily Support. Thus your Duty and Interest are always the same." HD, IX, 197-8 (TS, IV, 209).

are quixotic only in not being quixotic enough; they do not offer the vaguely idealistic appeal which men expect and perhaps welcome all the more because they need never expect to be able to meet it.[4] Third, the heroes of moderation demand, as they exhibit, an intense responsibility, a constant vigilance toward corruptions of institutions, of language, of reason. Because reason is present potentially in all men this kind of heroism is available to all. It is not a product of professional skill; it requires no prodigies of behavior, such as a laborer might need to compose an ode or to lead an army. Rather it demands of each man what he is by his nature prepared to supply, and the heroes may include a linen draper as readily as a nobleman. This leveling of the heroic ideal may deprive it of much of its apparent glory, especially since the most heroic exertions are no more than fulfillment of duty. As if to compensate, Swift places the lone hero against the odds of fashion and power—in fact, against noise and number.[5] In achieving his full humanity, he is opposed to the massed force of men who have surrendered theirs; in asserting truth, he is opposed to the clamor of manifold error. Yet even here not too much is to be claimed for the hero; he is not fighting lions but avoiding being devoured by rats. "I look upon myself," Swift wrote, "in the capacity of a clergyman, to be one appointed by Providence for defending a post assigned me, and for gaining over as many enemies as I can." [6]

The heroism of moderation is a way of dignifying the man who retains his rationality and resists the temptation to compete with animals in the desire for power. The animal myth is Swift's persistent device for portraying human irrationality in its horror: the young lady is warned against doing what monkeys can do better,[7] Gulliver is made to see that much of human glory is a more complex version of Yahoo brutality. The animal myth brings disgust to our recognition of the failure of humanity; the passions which cloud reason are uncomfortably parodied in

4. "Most things, pursued by men for the happiness of public or private life, our wit or folly have so refined, that they seldom subsist but in idea; a true friend, a good marriage, a perfect form of government, with some others, require so many ingredients, so good in their several kinds, and so much niceness in mixing them, that for some thousands of years men have despaired of reducing their schemes to perfection." *Hints towards an Essay on Conversation*, TS, XI, 67.

5. Cf. the allegorical contrast of false merit (born of Vanity and Impudence) with true (born of Virtue and Honour): "the Bastard Issue had a *loud shrill* Voice, which was perpetually employed in *Cravings* and *Complaints;* while the other never spoke louder than a *Whisper;* and was often so bashful that he could not speak at all." *Examiner*, No. 30 (1 March 1710), HD, III, 98–9 (TS, IX, 198). "I am apt to think, that Men of a great Genius are hardly brought to prostitute Pens in a very odious *Cause;* which, besides, is more properly undertaken by Noise and Impudence, by gross Railing and Scurrility, by Calumny and Lying, and by little trifling Cavils and Carpings in the wrong Place, which those *Whifflers* use for Arguments and Answers." *Examiner*, No. 19 (14 December 1710), HD, III, 36 (TS, IX, 115). Cf. also the remarks on "natural elocution," TS, XI, 73.

6. *Thoughts on Religion*, HD, IX, 262 (TS, III, 308).

7. *A Letter to a Very Young Lady on Her Marriage*, HD, XI, 91 (TS, XI, 120).

the appetites of animals. A stage beyond the beast lies simple mechanism, the reduction of man to matter in motion which Hobbes needed for a kind of political Newtonianism and which the moralist could turn into a satiric reduction. The compulsive acts of passion become the mechanical force of gravity, without the intrinsic horror of beasts' antics but even more devoid of human qualities and all the more startling as a contrast to man's claim to rationality. The satiric use of mechanism can combine with theodicy, as in Pope's *Essay on Man,* to show God's harmonious disposing in contrast to man's selfish proposing. The more man is led to greatness by irrational impulse the more readily he may fit into a cosmic order of which he is unaware. All this points to the constant emphasis, in Swift as well as Pope, on the need to remain human, to realize one's proper nature; in trying to become more than man, man inevitably becomes less. Extremes meet; high becomes low. The moment an impulsive act escapes rational control it is on the way to becoming matter in motion, just as in the absence of taste a poet may turn either to automatic writing or to the mechanical use of rules.

The versions of inhumanity all lead to what is perhaps Swift's central metaphor—the relation of outside to inside. The metaphor pervades the *Tale* and *Gulliver's Travels,* particularly as the problem of dress. The brothers of the *Tale* are fops, the Houyhnhnms are naked. Between the two lie most men—the decent Brobdingnagians, the modest Gulliver, the reformed Martin. The perfectly rational Houyhnhnms need no clothes; their bodies represent no challenge to their reason. For most men clothes are the necessary emblem of the *human* animal, the necessary restraint placed upon the passions of the body. To this extent clothes serve the ends of virtue; they are the necessary compromise between pure innocence and man's worst capabilities. Clothes in general show man's acceptance of his place in the natural order, neither beast nor angel, and man's particular dress signifies his rational acceptance of his proper place in a social order. The fop rebels against the social order in wearing clothes that are at once too grand for his proper station and too tasteless in their display to represent any proper place. He is not simply a commoner dressed as a lord; he is an amalgam of unrelated bits of finery. Clothes used in this way become an instrument not of decency or self-restraint but of conquest; in commanding attention and claiming prestige, they become the transparent expression of the body's appetites. Perfumes may adorn the body and conceal its rankness, but this is not restraint, as cleanliness would be. Sir John Davies wrote, "They smell best, that do of nothing smell," [8] and that is Swift's constant theme in his treatment

8. Sir John Davies, [*Nosce Teipsum*], *The Original, Nature, and Immortality of the Soul* (London, 1697), sec. xvii, p. 59. Swift read the poem in 1697; see *A Tale of a Tub,* ed. A. C. Guthkelch and D. N. Smith (Oxford, Clarendon Press, 1920), p. liii. The poem also supplies (p. 13) a more direct source than the Guthkelch-Smith edition indicates

of ladies' dressing rooms. The fop's clothes and the lady's perfumes represent on a small scale the mask of greatness used to hide a want of goodness.[9] There are three terms in the relationship—inside, outside, and the mediation of the two. In the fop the clothes fail to act as mediation or balance; the body has engrossed all control. In the Houyhnhnms mediation is unnecessary, for the body is docile. In the Yahoos it is totally neglected, for the rational soul is impotent. It is for good reason that Gulliver clings to his clothes as a mark of his difference from the Yahoo.

The metaphor of inside and outside extends far beyond the instance of dress. It is extended, for example, to all problems of manners. "Good breeding," as Swift defines it, is the dress of "good manners" and like all dress capable of usurping the end it should serve. A knowledge of forms can become a source of pedantic pride. One must live in the world, and Swift desires the young lady not "to be out of fashion, but to be the last and least in it." Finery is a "necessary folly," and the same is true of those "settled forms of general behaviour," arbitrary and irrational in themselves but necessary to the human animal as he is.[1] Nakedness is not for man, nor is society possible without ritual. Indeed, the man of moderation knows that "a little grain of the romance" may be a valuable corrective to man's inevitable component of brutality.[2] Jack, in the *Tale,* cannot be taught table manners, and the manners are important not merely as an allegorical account of the communion service but as a counterpart in the realm of polite conduct of the decency and modesty to be preserved in religious exercise. The man who makes of social intercourse an occasion for self-display or self-advancement is like the religious zealot who perverts doctrine to satisfy his own self-esteem or ambition. The love of novelty is a desire for distinction, and the self-seeker demands constant change—mercurial wit or revolving fashion—to maintain his superiority. Change for its own sake becomes the enemy of in-

---

(p. 80) for *"All in All, and All in every Part."* (Richard Mills has allowed me to use his copy of the 1697 edition, which, although it contains no marginal notes, has the signature "Jo :Swift" on the flyleaf.)

9. Cf. the *Examiner* on the Whigs: "Did these *Heroes* put off and lock up their *Virtues* when they came into Employment, and have they now resumed them since their Dismissions? If they wore them, I am sure it was *under* their *Greatness,* and without ever once convincing the World of their Visibility or Influence." *Examiner,* No. 26 (1 February 1710/1), HD, III, 78 (TS, IX, 169).

1. *A Treatise on Good Manners and Good Breeding,* TS, XI, 83–4; *Letter to a Very Young Lady,* HD, XI, 90–1 (TS, XI, 120–1). Cf also TS, I, 278: "It requires but little philosophy to discover and observe that there is no intrinsic value in all this; however, if it be founded in our nature, as an incitement to virtue, it ought not to be ridiculed."

2. "[A] little grain of the romance is no ill ingredient to preserve and exalt the dignity of human nature, without which it is apt to degenerate into everything that is sordid, vicious and low." *Hints towards an Essay on Conversation,* TS, XI, 74.

trinsic worth; it is better that man's conduct (or language or institutions) be imperfect than perpetually changing.[3]

The pattern which holds for manners holds as well for the institutions of church and state. The instruments of faith or of justice are easily turned into the instruments of power. We must learn "never to trust the execution of a law in the hands of those who will find it more to their interests to see it broken than observed." In Lilliput the laws are turned to travesty as the interests of the court dictate; among the Houyhnhnms laws are unnecessary; in Brobdingnag they are necessary and are saved from corruption by being made brief and universally comprehensible. If justice be opposed to partisan interest, the mixed state Swift favors is the only possibility of holding partisan interest in check; it allows justice to arise from the mutual limitations of king, lords, and commons. Such a state prevents a surrender to the unstable demands of either a capricious populace or a capricious monarch. Truth lies in the common agreements of opposed interests, in the interest of the whole rather than any part. The absolute monarch may be more efficient in achieving perfect justice, but the role demands a man of transcendent virtue, and it is too often played by a petty despot. Democracy presents the same dangers: it is a system that places power in the many, and the mere grouping of men into a mass brings the worst of them to the surface.[4] Again in the church the dangers of unlimited power in priesthood or laity are similar: on the one hand, Peter playing the charlatan; on the other, Jack deifying his own baseness.

If we generalize the pattern further we can see in Swift a concern which men have shown in all times—how to wed the timeless and the temporal, how to find

> the connection between
> The clock we are bound to obey
> And the miracle we must not despair of.[5]

For Swift the miracle is a daily possibility. The gifts of reason and of revelation make virtue attainable, but man is never free of the limitations of his nature. When he foolishly thinks that he can escape these limitations, his pride robs him of cautious responsibility and leaves him the victim of his passions and follies. Reason may be found in the rare man who is altogether free of private concerns and satisfying illusions; gen-

3. On language, see *A Proposal for Correcting, Improving, and Ascertaining the English Tongue*, TS, XI, 15. The warning of the *Examiner* is relevant here, as it is to *A Tale of a Tub*: "whatever be the Designs of innovating Men, they usually end in a Tyranny." *Examiner*, No. 39 (3 May 1711), HD, III, 146 (TS, IX, 260).

4. Cf. "the worst example, especially in a great majority, will certainly prevail." *An Essay on Modern Education*, TS, XI, 53. Cf. also "Paulus: An Answer," *Poems*, II, 435, lines 103–6.

5. W. H. Auden, *The Age of Anxiety* (New York, Random House, 1947), p. 134.

erally it is only to be found in the common beliefs of men through an infinite range of times and places. The concern with time runs through Swift's work in his constant appeals to posterity as the eventual restoration of reason, in his praise of Stella's endurance of spirit while time ravages her face ("So little is thy Form declin'd/Made up so largly in thy Mind" [6]), in his fear of change as the occasion of corruption. The timeless is single and simple, modest, and even invisible; opposed to it are motion, number, mechanical elaboration, "perpetual revolutions." Opposed to Stella's wit is the inanity of modern ladies; opposed to Martin's decency, the violence of Peter and Jack; opposed to cleanliness, finery and filth.

Yet the timeless must be embodied in the temporal; Swift's austerity is not a denial of the necessary folly, nor is it an ascetic impatience with human weakness. Devoted to the bagatelle, obviously capable of much half-bored playfulness, he shows sufficient compassion for other men's triviality. He seems austere only in recognizing the triviality for what it is; yet in doing so he has a way of describing it with sharpness and vigor. Like Pope's or even Dante's, his precision is the greater for his moral clarity, and if he is consistently unsentimental he is perhaps more genuinely charitable as a result. For many a satirist—one might compare Flaubert's dictionary of "idées reçues" with Swift's *Polite Conversation*—the failures of taste or good sense are fascinating disclosures of man's ineradicable foolishness. Swift never goes to the point of regarding the cackling of the hen or, much less, of revering it because it is accompanied with an egg. The temporal is necessary, for without it the timeless is inaccessible; yet it is to be controlled by the timeless, the body by the mind or soul, the institution by doctrine or principle, wit by reason or judgment.

Nowhere does Swift treat this problem of mediation with more delicacy than in *Cadenus and Vanessa*. In that poem Venus seeks to restore love to its proper condition, to rescue it from the sterile corruptions and make it once more

> *A Fire celestial, chaste, refin'd,*
> *Conceiv'd and kindled in the Mind.*

She creates an ideal woman in Vanessa, decent, modest, beautiful; by tricking Pallas she gains for her creature the wisdom generally granted only to men. The first reversal ensues: Vanessa is despised by both men and women.

> *To copy her, few Nymphs aspir'd;*
> *Her Virtues fewer Swains admir'd:*
> *So Stars beyond a certain Height*
> *Give Mortals neither Heat nor Light.*

6. "On Stella's Birthday" (1719), *Poems*, II, 722, lines 7–8.

To avenge his mother, Cupid inspires Vanessa with a love for her tutor Cadenus, and the second reversal is introduced. All her arts are now turned to winning her reluctant tutor; possessed by love, she can reason with a skill that defeats him at every turn. And just as the beaux were put off by the severity of Vanessa's good sense, so Cadenus is afraid of the passion she offers. He would prefer friendship—

> A constant, rational Delight,
> On Virtue's Basis fix'd to last,
> When Love's Allurements long are past;
> Which gently warms, but cannot burn.[7]

Cadenus' "exalted strains," however, do not move Vanessa; she will instruct him in those matters wherein the beau is far more skilled than he. There Swift allows the situation to stand. He has given to Vanessa both rationality and intensity of passion: the fools cannot respond to reason, the rational tutor cannot respond to passion. By attempting a freer celebration of passion than usual in Vanessa, Swift states the problem of divided man all the more effectively. Passion is not to be evaded by blunting Cupid's darts against Plutarch's *Morals*, as Cadenus tries to do. It may affect reason, but it need not undo it; Cadenus' incapacity for passion is as much a failure of humanity as the fop's rejection of celestial fire. Swift does not solve the problem; he explores it without too simple a commitment. To an extent Vanessa's passion makes her rhetoric more powerful than rational; to an extent Cadenus' inexperience in the ways of the beau is a mark of his superiority to human folly. But it is Vanessa who comes off the better; she is the woman who "never cou'd one Lover find" among the varieties of divided men. One can look back to Swift's ode to Temple, where the empire of unfallen virtue is the realm of the whole man. Or one can look ahead to Yeats' Crazy Jane:

> Love is all
> Unsatisfied
> That cannot take the whole
> Body and soul.[8]

Swift seems to have held to some belief in the existence of innate ideas. Probably he accepted the traditional doctrine he might have found, wherever else, in Sir John Davies—that the ideas cannot operate except for the occasions provided by the senses. As Socrates' questions might draw mathematical principles from Meno's slave boy, so the moralist's or the satirist's vision may awaken innate moral judgment. The

---

7. *Poems*, II, 687, lines 29–30; 700, lines 440–3; 711, lines 781–4. Cf. Swift's letter of courtship to Jane Waring (29 April 1696) : "Love, with the gall of too much discretion, is a thousand times worse than with none at all. It is a peculiar part of our nature which art debauches, but cannot improve." *Correspondence*, I, 20.

8. W. B. Yeats, "Crazy Jane on the Day of Judgment" ("Words for Music Perhaps," III), *Collected Poems* (New York, Macmillan, 1941), p. 295.

principles are recollected only through experience, and they must in turn be applied to new experience with caution and tact. Most men are easily ruled by the appearance of good; but the appearance may be a fair out-side concealing rottenness. The Tale Teller is willing to throw up his hands, to assure us that the outside is always preferable to the inside, only to have us surrender our critical concern and accept the superficial. The surface is what strikes the senses. The senses give us happiness. Why trouble ourselves about virtue? The moralist, as the Tale Teller sees him, is a mangler and flayer who can never be happy. Swift's own solu-tion is not "to sodder and patch up" the flaws of the surface, to erect a theodicy that absolves us of responsibility.[9] This would be, in the style of the *Tale,* to invest the universe with a "macro-coat." The task, instead, is one of examining the motives and the consequences of our behavior, of making explicit what our conduct implies.

For all the system building of theologians and the complacency of rationalistic divines, the task of discrimination remains: "by pretending by the Lines and Measures of our Reason, to extend the Dominion of one invisible Power, and contract that of the other, [we] have discov-ered a gross Ignorance in the Natures of Good and Evil, and most hor-ribly confounded the Frontiers of both. . . . Thus do Men establish a Fellowship of *Christ* with *Belial.*"[1] It is this confusion of good and evil that all of Swift's work is designed to meet. Since the inside cannot be seen directly, we are all of us in this respect "reasoners at a distance," comparing profession with achievement, testing the accuracy of terms, simplifying by appropriate analogy. True wit is the bridge between the rationally intuited truth and the evidence of our senses; it gives the truth concrete application, and it shapes our experience in turn by rational principles. In a sense it provides, as Sidney recognized, "a true lively knowledge," more subtle and complex than the simple awareness of fact or principle, of particular or general alone. Since wit relates inside and outside as life does not, it has the surprise of novelty. With its aid the outside may suddenly become transparent and turn out to be like Dry-den's helmet when the vizard was lifted: "For, the Helmet was nine times too large for the Head, which appeared Situate far in the hinder Part, even like the Lady in a Lobster, or like a Mouse under a Canopy of State, or like a shrivled Beau, from within the Pent-House of a mod-ern Perewig."[2] Or the benevolent principles may prove to have been

9. Cf. the lines on the knave who cheats his lord: "He knows a Thousand Tricks, whene'er he please,/Though not to cure, yet palliate each Disease." "To Mr. Gay," *Poems,* II, 535, lines 123–4. Cf. also John Tillotson, *Works* (London, 1696), p. 373: "men had rather that Religion should be any thing than what it is . . . And therefore they had much rather have something that might handsomely palliate and excuse their evil inclinations and practices, than to be obliged to retrench and renounce them."
1. *The Mechanical Operation of the Spirit,* HD, I, 179–80 (TS, I, 199–200).
2. *The Battle of the Books,* HD, I, 157 (TS, I, 179).

applied without a full awareness of fact and may turn into a "modest proposal."

Swift gave to modern criticism the term "vehicle," and no one has so carefully explored the relation of the vehicle to what it contains, of the periwig to the beau. His methods as stylist and satirist are devices for dissociating the apparent from the real, and the dissociation is made only to prepare us for giving the real its proper residence in, and control over, appearance. It is all-important that man should *see* clearly, should detect the serpent in the brass, on the one hand, or the timeless law in the temporal occasion, on the other. Therefore Swift is always asking the reader that most disarming of questions: "Is this an Age of the World to think Crimes improbable because they are great?" [3]

3. *Some Remarks upon a Pamphlet, Entitl'd a Letter to the Seven Lords,* HD, III, 190 (TS, V, 37).

Index

N